D0617969

Short + Sweet
Gale gand

Out	Name	In

Lory Smith
19301 Ponderosa Dr
Weston, CO 81091-9742

GALE GAND'S

short

+

sweet

GALE GAND'S
short
+
sweet

{quick desserts
with eight ingredients
or less

GALE GAND + JULIA MOSKIN

Photographs by Tim Turner

Clarkson Potter/Publishers
New York

This book is dedicated to

* My delightful husband, Jimmy, for thinking clearly when I can't, for having the power to calm me when I'm anxious and on deadline, for brewing me another cup of tea, for always making me feel I'm the most beautiful and greatest cook there is when our family sits down at the table to eat, and for holding my coat through our poetic, sweet, inspirational life together. You are such a gift.
* My lovely, funny, smart son, Gio, for enriching my life and bringing me such joy in and out of the kitchen.
* And my mother, Myrna, for the cold, precise hands you gave me that love and live to make pie crust after pie crust with Great-Grandma's rolling pin. I'm doing it with Gio now using rhubarb from my garden, only I'm you and he's me—boy, do I miss you.

Copyright © 2004 by Gale's Bread and Butter, Inc., and Julia Moskin
Photographs copyright © 2004 by Tim Turner

All rights reserved. No part of this book may be reproduced or transmitted in any form or by any means, electronic or mechanical, including photocopying, recording, or by any information storage and retrieval system, without permission in writing from the publisher.

Published by Clarkson Potter/Publishers, New York, New York.
Member of the Crown Publishing Group, a division of Random House, Inc.
www.crownpublishing.com

CLARKSON N. POTTER is a trademark and POTTER and colophon are registered trademarks of Random House, Inc.

Printed in Singapore

Design by Jane Treuhaft

Library of Congress Cataloging-in-Publication Data is available upon request.

ISBN 1-4000-4733-1

10 9 8 7 6 5 4 3 2

First Edition

acknowledgments

Thanks to:

* Julia Moskin for giving us a voice and for friendship
* Jane Dystel for watching over us and taking care of things
* Tim Turner for catching the beauty of food on film
* Roy Finamore for making the process easy
* Pam Krauss for adopting us
* Mary Anne Forness for testing and testing
* My dad, Bob, for working so hard to live so long to be here for us all
* Aunt Lana for never being all out of time
* Vita Seidita and family for cooking with me and sharing their family heirloom recipes
* Fran Seidita for all that Cameoware
* Grandma Elsie Grossman for leaving me her recipe card files, and so organized!
* Aunt Greta and Uncle Robert for supporting my cooking and the ham—oh my God, that ham!
* Uncle Jack and Aunt Judy for digging up old family recipe cards and mailing them to me
* Rick Tramonto for being a great culinary partner
* Rich Melman for being a great business partner
* TV Food Network for making me feel more like a star than anyone deserves
* Julia Child for including me
* Judy Anderson, Karen Katz, and Ina Pinkney for holding my hand, always
* My entire staff and partners at Tru and Lettuce Entertain You, Enterprises
* Larry Binstein and European Imports for cheese and dairy products and selling my root beer
* Filbert's Bottling Company for co-packing my root beer
* Swan Creek Farms and George Rasmussen for organic eggs, honey, and maple syrup for my pastries
* New Leaf and Bukiety for blooms for the book and our restaurant
* Tekla Incorporated and Sofia Solomon for beautiful cheeses
* Heartland Trading's American Cheese Collection and Giles Schnierle for farmhouse Cheddar and other wonderful things
* Farmer Jones and family for the best soil, the best herbs, and micro greens
  —**Gale Gand**

I still can't thank Gale enough for taking a chance on me four (!) books ago. This one is for Darren and for Billy, the best thing we've cooked together yet.
—**Julia Moskin**

contents

*introduction

How often do you hear yourself saying things like: "I'm totally frantic today" or "We're having a crazy week!" or "Where does the time go?" We all seem to be a little too busy these days. I try to remember that a complicated life is also a blessing. I love my family, my work, my house and garden, my friends, and my cats and dog! Even though all together, they make for a demanding life schedule, I wouldn't have things any other way. I suspect most of you feel the same way.

Like other working parents (and to me, that includes *all* parents), I struggle with having time for the things I *have* to do and the things I *want* to do. For many of us, cooking from scratch is no longer something we *have* to do. Our supermarkets are stocked with complete chicken dinners, precooked pasta, and huge salad bars. Bakeries provide us with fresh bread, cookies, and birthday cakes.

But home cooking is still something I *want* to do, for myself and my family. You'd think that as a chef, it would be easy for me—but my schedule keeps me out of my own kitchen as much as anyone. Believe it or not, I *do* understand how it feels to have no time to cook!

When I was lucky enough to become the host of a daily dessert show on the Food Network, my schedule really got pushed to the limit. I thought I'd never have time for home cooking again. But I still want my son to eat cookies that I have baked just for him, not only the best ones I can buy. I want to sit down with my husband, even if it's only once a week, to a meal that we have made for ourselves right down to the dessert. When I manage to bring a homemade sweet to a friend's house-warming or baby shower, I like knowing I made the effort to bake it myself, even if it's the simplest possible coffee cake or fruit crisp.

So, as my life has become more full and rich, my desserts have had to become more simple. At Tru, the elegant fine-dining mecca in Chicago where I am the pastry chef (and a partner in running the restaurant), my team and I still enjoy spinning wild variations on sweet themes. But for myself, and for the thousands of Americans who watch me cook on TV, home desserts mean simple desserts.

The good news is: Simple doesn't mean boring.

Simple doesn't have to mean the same old pound cake or chocolate chip cookies or a basic apple pie, good as those things can be. Simple can mean intense flavor and stylish presentations. Simple can mean a jolt of surprise, an "oh, I never thought of putting those two things together" moment that makes the easiest dessert taste fresh and lively. Simple means big flavor: making powerful tastes like coconut, cocoa, or peanut butter work for you, for example, or using buttery croissants as the base for bread pudding. Simple means making the most of the seasons, letting juicy-

fresh peaches, pears, or figs speak for themselves with just a little prompting. Simple means buying top-notch ingredients, from chocolate to cream to raspberries, that need just a hug and a kiss to make them table-ready.

More good news: You don't have to have the knife skills or kitchen versatility of an Iron Chef to make desserts that beat the clock. Here's the main thing you have to do in order to cook quickly: Think ahead, whether it's a matter of shopping in advance or making a dessert beforehand up until the final step. That's what we chefs do. Making dinner for hundreds of people every night means that we have to make lots of things in advance, then finish them at the last minute. You can, too. In many of the recipes that follow, it's those last five minutes that really produce the dessert.

Grilled Pecorino with Fresh Figs and Honey; see recipe on page 54.

So, each recipe includes a detailed breakdown of what you can do ahead of time—sometimes days or even weeks ahead! In almost every case, you can produce a flawless dessert for six people with no more than ten minutes of last-minute activity in the kitchen. I've reduced each recipe to numbered steps, then looked at each step to see how it could be streamlined. I know that even a simple-looking step can take a long time if you need to get another pan off the rack, another spice out of the cupboard, or another size of measuring spoon out from the drawer. And I also know that every additional mixing bowl or utensil you use can mean more time at the sink, so I've tried to keep tools to a minimum.

Another way to keep dessert quick is to limit the number of ingredients you work with. Fans and friends tell me that for home cooks, getting your ingredients together and measuring them out is often the most time-consuming part of cooking. So, I decided that no recipe in this book would call for more than eight ingredients. Many recipes don't even have that many: Cherry Clafouti, Orange Panna Cotta, and Dulce de Leche on Toasted Pound Cake all come in under par. Water is the only ingredient that doesn't count toward the total.

By testing these recipes on home cooks, I've made sure that most of the recipes will have you in and out of the kitchen in thirty minutes or less. The recipes are divided into chapters according to how much *active* time you can expect to spend in the kitchen. Each recipe was tested for timing, but does not include the time a sorbet will need to harden in the freezer, or the time a cake will spend in the oven. So as always, read the recipe all the way through before you start.

I'm very excited for you to cook from this book. This is the book that my friends (and fans) have been asking me to write; it's the book that truly lets you get a home-made dessert on the table fast, even on a busy weeknight. Some are classic desserts of the home kitchen, taste-tested and time-tested, like angel food cake, shortbread, and pudding—but with new flavor sparks like fresh berries, a touch of espresso, even fragrant buds of dried lavender. Others are favorite speedy innovations from my restaurant kitchen, like Banana Bisque, Deep Chocolate Terrine, and Roasted Peaches with Thyme and Ricotta.

Many of the recipes are simple and quick enough to make with kids around. Cooking with my son, Gio, is one of the great pleasures of my life, and it has nothing to do with the fact that I am a professional chef! Yes, he thinks that I am a miraculously good cook—but remember, to small children, all cooking is somewhat miraculous. They all think their parents are expert cooks, even if all you can make is chocolate chip cookies and pancakes. Baking buttermilk biscuits or chocolate pudding from scratch, or making caramel corn and choosing a surprise to put in each bag, are fun projects that can introduce your kids to the pleasures of the kitchen—and, if necessary, fill up a whole rainy afternoon or snow day. The chapter titled "Kids in the Kitchen" focuses on recipes that kids can make mostly on their own, or that grownups might not be too tempted by (like Peanut Butter Worms).

When Gio was small (he's seven now), one of the first rituals that we fell into was cooking weekend breakfasts together. As soon as he was old enough to stand on a stool at the kitchen counter, he "helped" stir batter for the pancakes we'd make from my mother's recipe. These days, he can almost make "Grandma Myrna pancakes" by himself, and he has developed a lot of cooking skills and even his own recipes. We try to go to the farmer's market once a week, and together we invent dishes to use up the produce we buy, from farmers he knows by name. He knows that apples come in the fall and peaches in the summer. He tells me when it's time to stock up on more of the spicy fennel sausage that our friend, chef Mario Batali, sends to us. All of this brings us closer to each other, to the big outside world, and to the earth.

Cooking, with kids or without, can be a wonderful combination of the practical and the recreational. Once you break out of your old standbys, you'll find a lively new world of flavor and color and texture and aroma. And I hope these recipes will be the inspiration to get you there!

tips + basics

My "Rules" for Quick Desserts

* **The better your ingredients are, the less you have to do to them.** Starting with ripe fruit, top-quality chocolate, fresh butter, pure extracts, and organic eggs and milk will take you a long way toward your goal of making delicious desserts quickly.

* **Let the cooking tools do the work for you.** Have on hand simple tools like a *sharp* peeler, a good grater/zester (I love the Microplane ones), top-quality non-stick baking pans or mats, and a mixing bowl that can also act as the top of a double boiler: Each one can shave minutes off your prep and cleanup time.

* **A standing mixer frees up your hands** for other jobs, which speeds the cooking process.

* Be like the pros and **use your large, sharp knives** (not little paring knives) for chopping jobs. You'll get more done with each swipe of the knife.

* A lot of time can be saved simply by **keeping your baking essentials at hand,** instead of stuffed into an inaccessible closet or drawer. If nothing else, at least keep a sheet pan, a 9-inch cake pan, and your mixer nearby. You can make almost any dessert in this book just with those. Sometimes having lots of equipment can slow you down. A tip from a friend that I've found useful: Tack a small ruler to the shelf where you keep your baking pans, so you can quickly measure them and eliminate the guesswork.

* **Do use baking shortcuts** such as premade puff pastry, canned and frozen prepared fruits, and even frozen pie crust. Sure, homemade pie crust is best—but it's better to use frozen than to skip making dessert. We're all more likely to cook when we don't have to start from the very beginning; the feeling that some of the work has already been done can be all it takes to get you into the kitchen.

* **Stop shopping.** Many of you tell me that it's the time spent shopping for ingredients, more than the time spent cooking in the kitchen, that prevents you from baking as often as you'd like. So don't! Keep butter, sugar, flour, eggs, milk, vanilla

extract, chocolate, cinnamon, and coffee always on hand. Stash away some nuts, dried fruit, flaked coconut, dry gelatin, baking soda, and baking powder in a cupboard. You have the makings of countless desserts right there. And then if you just need a pint of berries or a few limes to complete a recipe, the shopping will take five minutes instead of twenty-five.

The following are my general guidelines for smooth sailing in the kitchen. They will help you work comfortably and efficiently with your ingredients and equipment, which is the true key to cooking quickly. But throughout the book, you'll also find my "quick tricks;" the little shortcuts and tips on speeding things up in the kitchen that I've developed over twenty years of cooking for hundreds of people every day!

Chocolate

Buying Although you don't have to buy the most expensive European chocolate, I do recommend that you use baking chocolate rather than chocolate chips or bars in my recipes, especially when the chocolate will be melted. Chocolate chips can be very good, but they contain additives that help them keep their shape—the opposite of what you want melted chocolate to do. American brands of chocolate like Scharffen Berger and Ghirardelli are very good, and Valrhona and Callebaut are even better. Fine baking chocolate is really designed to be smoother and easier to work with, and the flavor alone can be worth the extra money. Bottom line: Use the best chocolate you can afford, and save on other baking products by buying generic brands.

Melting I feel that the good old double-boiler method can't be beat. Start with chopped chocolate (see below) for even melting. The trick is to adjust the heat so that the water in the bottom is barely simmering, not bubbling or boiling. The simmer should be just visible; French cooks call this stage "smiling." Chocolate melted over barely simmering water will not scorch, so you can leave it in the bowl until you need it. If you don't have a double boiler, set a metal or heat-proof glass bowl over a saucepan with an inch or so of water in the bottom. The bottom of the bowl should not be touching the water. Stir frequently. Never cover chocolate in a double boiler, even after it is melted. Drops of water might form on the lid, and if they drop into the chocolate, it may seize up and stiffen.

If you prefer the microwave, put the chocolate in a glass bowl and microwave at medium power for 1 minute. Stir, then repeat, checking and stirring the chocolate every 30 seconds. To avoid scorching, stop when there are still a few lumps of chocolate left, and melt them by stirring them into the melted chocolate.

Melt white chocolate slowly in a double boiler over steaming hot water; do not let the water simmer. White chocolate scorches at a lower temperature than regular chocolate.

Chopping To chop chocolate, use a large serrated knife and have your chocolate at room temperature. Cold chocolate is too hard to cut, and the knife can slip and cut you. Room-temperature chocolate will chop into pieces, and will not splinter and fly around the kitchen. To chop chocolate in a food processor, chill your chocolate, work bowl, and blade first, then pulse the chocolate just until chopped.

Storing Store your chocolate at room temperature, not in the refrigerator. Storing chocolate in the refrigerator encourages it to "bloom;" the cocoa butter starts to separate out and shows up as a fine white cloud on the surface of the chocolate. Bloomed chocolate, although it looks funny, is perfectly usable and will taste fine; melting it will bring the elements back together.

Cocoa I know there's a lot of confusion out there about cocoa. The most important thing about it is: Cocoa is not the same thing as hot cocoa mix or any sweetened chocolate powder. Cocoa is a pure, unsweetened powder made by grinding the hard "nibs" derived from the cocoa bean where most of the chocolate flavor is found. (This is also the first step in making chocolate.) As with chocolate, you don't have to buy the fancy stuff, but once you try it you will taste and see the difference. Valrhona, Ghirardelli, and Scharffen Berger all make delicious cocoas.

Some cocoa, like Droste and some Hershey's cocoa, is "Dutched." This refers to a process invented in Holland whereby the cocoa is treated to neutralize its acid content and make it smoother in flavor. It's really a matter of taste; some "gourmet" cocoa is Dutched, but some manufacturers feel that the untreated cocoa is purer. Both kinds can be very good.

The one place where Dutching really matters is when baking with baking soda. Cocoa that is not Dutched, and therefore has a higher acid content, turns deep red when you combine it with alkaline baking soda (that's how Red Velvet cake originally got its color).

Butter

Salted vs Unsalted Unsalted butter is usually preferred in cooking, because it tends to be fresher (unsalted butter does not last as long as salted butter, which means that markets have to turn over their supply more often). But since the salt is a natural preservative, salted butter lasts longer in the refrigerator, making it a convenient choice for some cooks. I always buy unsalted butter and keep it in the freezer until I need it. Then I add salt to my recipe (which may seem strange, but a little salt is very important in sweet recipes: it really brings out the flavors).

If substituting one for the other, the proportion to remember is one stick of butter takes about ⅛ teaspoon of salt. Add or subtract pinches of salt in the recipe accordingly. To keep to my eight-ingredient rule for this book, I've used salted butter a bit more than I usually would.

Creaming Remove your butter from the refrigerator 30 minutes before trying to cream it. If you are starting with frozen butter, cut it into pieces and give it at least 45 minutes at room temperature to warm up. Microwaving butter to warm it quickly doesn't really work; it goes from frozen butter directly to melted butter. What you want is *cool* butter. Butter has been correctly creamed when it is smooth, not when it is clumped up on your mixer beaters. If it clumps, it's still too cold; give it a few more minutes to soften while you do something else. Or, you can just keep mixing it: The warmth and friction created by the mixing will soften the butter quickly. You want a soft, fluffy paste of cool butter, made lighter than what you began with from the air you've mixed in. This is an integral step in many recipes, so don't skimp on it! If it seems to be getting too greasy and warm, simply stick it back in the refrigerator for a few minutes after creaming.

Egg Whites

Separating eggs is easier when they are cold. Refrigerate the yolks after separating, but let the whites warm up slightly before whipping them. They will be stiffer and fluffier, and if you are folding them into temperature-sensitive ingredients like melted chocolate it's best if they are not cold. Whip them in a completely clean, completely dry bowl; a speck of yolk, water, or grease can make it impossible to whip whites stiff. Whip egg whites at high speed in a large bowl, to get the most air into them. I often whip them to the soft peak stage, then add a little sugar for the final minute of whipping. The sugar dissolves and helps the egg whites stiffen without breaking.

Egg whites can be frozen very successfully. I freeze them individually in ice cube trays, then pop them out into resealable plastic bags. Thaw them at room temperature as needed.

Toasting Nuts and Coconut

Toasting is an important step for releasing and deepening the flavors. Use this method for whole or coarsely chopped nuts, sesame seeds, or flaked coconut. Spread the nuts out in a single layer on a baking sheet and put them in a preheated 350-degree oven (or toaster oven). Check them frequently after the first 5 minutes, and stir every 5 minutes to make sure they brown evenly. When they smell toasty and look golden and slightly browned, after 10 to 20 minutes, remove them immediately; they will continue cooking a bit as they cool. If they are very brown already, transfer to a cool pan or spread out on a plate, as they can scorch in the hot pan even when they are out of the oven. Don't try to toast ground nuts; they will burn.

Before chopping toasted nuts, let them cool completely or they may be too oily to chop. You can pulse them in a food processor, pulsing just until coarse crumbs form (watch closely: it's easy to overprocess and find yourself with nut paste) or chop them coarsely with a large, sharp knife.

Toasting Spices and Seeds

Toasting cinnamon sticks, cloves, cardamom seeds, and such to release their flavor is best done on top of the stove. Heat a small skillet, then pour in the seeds and toss them until fragrant. Immediately remove from the skillet and let cool before using.

Phyllo Dough

Phyllo dough is mostly available frozen, and it is of very good quality. Try to buy it from a store that has high turnover, as long freezing can dry out the phyllo and make the sheets stick together. The day before you plan to use it, put it in the refrigerator to thaw. Fresh phyllo should be stored in the refrigerator.

When ready to work, spread the stack of phyllo out on a work surface and cover it with a tea towel. Phyllo is very thin, but if you work it gently you will not have any problems—and a few small tears don't matter. To remove one sheet, first lift up each of the four corners to loosen them. Then run your fingers underneath the whole sheet before lifting it up by two corners. Don't try to peel a sheet off by one corner like shelf paper; the phyllo will tear. Once you have removed as many sheets as you need for the time being, cover the stack again with the towel to prevent it from drying out.

Puff Pastry

Frozen puff pastry is an excellent and convenient product to keep in the house. Thaw it in the refrigerator for several hours or overnight. When you unfold it on a work surface, run a rolling pin over it to smooth out any creases or cracks. As you work with it, if it seems to be getting limp or sticky, put it back in the fridge for 15 minutes to firm up.

Simple Syrup

This clear syrup of sugar and water is a useful ingredient to have in the refrigerator, especially in the summer when iced teas and lemonades call for sweetening. It also comes in handy when you don't want the grittiness of sugar in a recipe. To make it, combine equal parts sugar and water in a saucepan and bring to a boil. Boil 1 minute, then let cool. Kept refrigerated, simple syrup will last indefinitely.

Pastry Bags

A pastry bag is simply a cone of canvas with an open end for squeezing batters, frostings, and soft doughs (the process is called "piping" in dessert language). A 14-inch model will be able to handle most any recipe you will make. Fit one of the removable metal tips into the end, fill the bag, and off you go.

To fill a pastry bag, first fit in the tip. If your batter is soft and you feel that it might ooze out the bottom, pinch the bag closed with a clothespin just above the tip. Fold down the top edge of the bag all the way around to form a collar, prop the pastry bag up (a large coffee can, tall canister, or vase works well for this), and fill, gently pressing the filling down into the bag to eliminate air pockets. Or you can hold your hand like a C and hold the bag, resting the collar on your thumb and forefinger, using the other hand to fill. Unfold the collar, twist the top closed, and secure it until you are ready to pipe.

However, you don't need a "real" pastry bag to pipe. Thick resealable plastic bags make great pastry bags—in fact, they have certain advantages over professional ones. With a plastic bag, you fill the bag and seal it shut. When you're ready to pipe, you just snip off a corner and go. You can even use a pinking shears to cut the corner, making a star tip that will produce a more decorative effect.

Piping itself looks slightly intimidating but is incredibly easy to do. To hold your filled pastry bag, twist the material just above the filling. Remove the clothespin, if you're using one. Hold the twist closed with one hand and put the other hand below it, wrapping your fingers around the filled bag as though you are holding a baseball bat. The bottom hand guides and steadies, as the top hand squeezes the filling down.

As you pipe, you may need to stop occasionally and slide your fingers down the length of the bag to push the filling down. Retwist the top of the bag just above the filling before continuing to pipe.

It's best to pipe batters and doughs into the pans as soon as possible after you make them. Once they're in the pans, though, many desserts can be held at room temperature or in the refrigerator until you are ready to bake.

Most cloth pastry bags are coated with plastic on the inside to make them easier to use and clean. Coated pastry bags can be turned inside out and washed in the dishwasher; so can resealable plastic bags.

Cookie Sheets

The technology for nonstick cookie sheets just keeps getting better, and they are good for most everything. But this is a case where quality counts: Professional-quality, heavyweight nonstick sheets really work better than lightweight inexpensive versions. Buy the best ones you feel you can afford. Cheaper ones may need a coat of butter over the surface to make them truly nonstick.

Since I use hundreds of aluminum sheet pans in my restaurant kitchen, that's what I'm used to. I start with heavy cookie sheets, the light silver-gray type. For lining the cookie sheets, I almost always choose no-fuss parchment paper, which you can buy at most supermarkets and all baking supply stores. It can be reused a few times if it's not sticky or burnt. Cookies and meringues slide easily off its surface, and you can lift a whole sheet's worth off the pan at once, instead of chasing them down one by one with a spatula.

To line a pan with parchment, cut a sheet the same size as the bottom of your pan, then swipe a little butter around the edges and make an X of butter across the center. Lay the sheet in the pan and press to adhere to the butter. The butter makes the paper hold on to the pan surface, which is especially important when you're piping onto the paper; otherwise, the paper will irritate you by lifting up from the pan as you pipe. Wax paper can also be used, using the unwaxed side as your baking surface. I also use parchment and wax paper for lining loaf pans and sheet cake pans.

Even better for many purposes are the new rubberized silicone mats that some bakeware dealers are importing from Europe; look for names like Silpat and Matfer. You can buy them at Amazon.com and at Williams-Sonoma. They are especially effective when making sweets with a high sugar content, like tuiles and candies. *Nothing* sticks to them, and you can simply lay them on the cookie sheet. They are easy to wipe clean, and you don't need to wash the pan underneath.

Ramekins

A ramekin is just a flat-bottomed, straight-sided cup, made of sturdy ceramic and with a ribbed or smooth outside surface—much like a miniature soufflé dish. Ramekins are extremely useful both for baking and for making individual desserts that require refrigeration or freezing, like puddings and custards. However, any dessert that is simply going to be chilled—not baked—can also be made in a decorative demitasse cup, teacup, cordial cup, or anything else that takes your fancy.

Pastry Brushes

Pastry brushes can be flat or round, and can be bought at many supermarkets and all baking supply stores. I don't recommend using hardware-store brushes, even the natural bristle ones, unless you are sure that the bristles haven't been chemically treated. It's good to have a small one and a larger one for desserts, and to keep them separate from brushes you use with savory food. One garlic marinade is all it takes to flavor a pastry brush for a long, long time!

To clean pastry brushes, I wash them well in soap and the hottest water I can find; use boiling water if your tap water isn't steaming hot. Then I dry them quickly by placing them on top of the oven or dishwasher, or another warm surface. They can take a long time to dry completely; if you put them away damp they may begin to mildew.

Double Boilers

A double boiler is extremely useful for melting chocolate and cooking custards and fillings. But I have to admit that I rarely use mine; instead, I set a metal or heat-proof glass bowl on top of a saucepan of water. In many cases the bowl can do double duty as the mixing bowl for the recipe.

Zesters

I use a lot of lemon and orange zest in my cooking, and the new generation of Microplane zesters—the ones adapted from woodworking tools—has really changed my life. They are available at cookware stores and from some catalogs. They create a feathery, fine zest with very little mess or effort.

However, a small, flat cheese grater or a carefully wielded vegetable peeler with sharp blades will also work well. If using a vegetable peeler, cut only the colored part off the fruit, then mince the pieces into small shreds. Always avoid scraping any of the white pith into your zest.

Ice-Cream Scoops

Ice-cream scoops have many more uses in the kitchen than serving ice cream. For baking, buy the kind with a swiping blade that scrapes the scoop clean each time; you'll need it for sticky batters and doughs. I always use them for filling muffin cups with batter, making biscuits (see the recipe for Killer Buttermilk Biscuits, page 147), and even scooping cookie dough onto baking sheets; they ensure that each scoop is the same size. You can buy them in many sizes at baking supply stores: The small ones are perfect for cookie dough.

When you are scooping cookie dough, level off the scoop with a knife before swiping it, so that you'll have a flat bottom to place the cookie on.

Kitchen Scissors

Any pair of sturdy scissors with stainless, washable blades can be used in the kitchen. I use them mostly for snipping dried fruit into manageable pieces: They work better than a knife on anything sticky. For baking, you don't need super-strong kitchen shears, which can be quite expensive.

Water Baths

To make a hot-water bath, or *bain-marie*, line a roasting pan that's at least 2 inches deep with paper towels or newspapers. This is to create a layer of water *under* the baking dish as well as around it; direct contact between the metal roasting pan and the baking dish would create a "hot spot" where they meet. Also, the paper will keep the dish or dishes from sliding around. Arrange the dish or dishes in the roasting pan, leaving room between them and making sure they are not touching the sides of the pan. Then fill the pan with very hot tap water until it comes halfway up the sides of the dishes. Place the pan in a preheated oven; the temperature is given in the recipe.

To make an ice bath, fill a large bowl with ice cubes, then add cold water just to cover. The mixture should be mostly ice to create the cooling power you want. When you rest a bowl in the ice water, the contents will cool down very quickly as long as you stir it often.

15-minute recipes

deep chocolate terrine

This almost instant recipe produces dense bites of pure chocolate that melt on the tongue. This is wonderful with unsweetened or flavored whipped cream, garnished with whole raspberries or candied orange peel, or utterly plain. The almond spikes take about 30 minutes to make and are very pretty, but entirely optional.

When chilled, the cake will be firm enough to slice. You might also cut the slices into shapes with a cookie cutter. Dip your cutter in hot water between cuts for smooth, clean results. If you would prefer a thin sheet of cake to a loaf, bake the recipe in an 8-inch square pan, reducing the baking time by about 5 minutes.

MAKES 10 SERVINGS

For the terrine
8 ounces best-quality semisweet
    chocolate
12 tablespoons (1½ sticks)
    unsalted butter
¾ cup sugar
½ cup strong brewed coffee
4 eggs, well beaten

For the almond spikes (optional)
1 cup sugar
¼ cup water
20 whole blanched almonds,
    lightly toasted (see page 17)

1. At least 1 day before serving, make the terrine: Line a loaf pan with aluminum foil. Prepare a hot-water bath (see page 23). Heat the oven to 350 degrees.

2. Melt the chocolate and butter together in a double boiler or a bowl set over barely simmering water. Add the sugar and coffee and heat through, stirring often. When the mixture is hot, whisk well to dissolve the sugar. In a separate bowl, whisk the eggs. Remove the chocolate mixture from the heat and whisk in the eggs.

3. Pour the mixture into the loaf pan and bake in the hot-water bath for 40 minutes. Let cool to room temperature, then refrigerate overnight.*

4. Make the almond spikes: Pour the sugar into the center of a deep saucepan. Carefully pour the water around the walls of the pan, trying not to splash any sugar onto the walls. Do not stir; gently draw your finger twice through the center of the sugar, making a cross, to moisten it. Over high heat, bring to a full boil and cook without stirring until light amber in color, 5 to 10 minutes. Test the color by pouring drops onto a white plate (remember that the caramel will continue to cook slightly as it cools down, so stop the cooking when the mixture is a few shades lighter than amber).

5. Meanwhile, stick a toothpick into the broad end of each almond. Place two sticks of cold butter or a big piece of hard cheese on a shelf over a counter, lining up the edge of the butter with the edge of the shelf. Place a piece of wax paper or paper towel on the counter to catch any drips. (You can also do this on the edge of the counter, placing the paper on the kitchen floor.)

6. When the caramel is done, turn off the heat and let cool a few minutes until it is slightly viscous. Dip an almond in the caramel, then stick the toothpick in the butter with the almond sticking out over the counter. The caramel will drip down and make a strand as it cools, which takes just a few minutes. Make batches of about 8 almonds; by the time you stick the last one in the butter, the first one will have cooled. As they cool, remove them from the butter and stack them in an airtight container, with wax paper between the layers.** (To wash the saucepan, soak it overnight.)

7. When ready to serve, turn the terrine out onto a serving platter. Cut into slices for serving, or see above for other suggestions. Remove the toothpicks from the almond spikes and use them to garnish each serving, with the caramel spikes sticking up.

 * *The terrine can be refrigerated for up to 3 days, or frozen for up to 3 weeks.*

** *The almonds should be served the same day they are made.*

honey-toasted crumpets
with golden fruit compote

Crumpets are an English teatime treat—little griddle cakes that you toast (in English children's books, they are always doing this with long forks over the nursery fire) and then soak with butter and honey. I grew addicted to tea and crumpets when I lived in England. So I've been delighted to find crumpets in American supermarkets, usually in vacuum-sealed packages in the bread aisle. This is a great, quick, winter afternoon snack or brunch treat.

I created this low-fat dish for my always health-conscious dad, Bob. He wouldn't slather butter on the crumpets, but I probably would! For a creamier treat, you can serve this with dollops of vanilla yogurt; for a more pungent one, I like to eat it with shards of aged, sharp Cheddar cheese.

MAKES 3 TO 6 SERVINGS

For the compote
1½ **cups golden raisins or dried**
   cherries
1½ **cups dried apricots, quartered with**
   kitchen scissors
¾ **cup sugar**
2 **cinnamon sticks or 2 teaspoons star**
   anise pods (broken ones are fine)
1 **vanilla bean, split lengthwise**

For serving
6 **crumpets (see head note)**
2 **tablespoons honey**
2 **tablespoons butter (optional)**

1. Make the compote: Combine the raisins, apricots, sugar, cinnamon, and vanilla bean in a saucepan with 1 cup water and bring to a simmer. Cook for 10 minutes, then turn off the heat and let the fruit plump for at least 30 minutes.*

2. When ready to serve, toast the crumpets and spread with the honey and butter (if using). If you are using a toaster oven, put the crumpets back in and toast again, just until the honey is bubbly and the surface is golden brown. Place each crumpet on a plate and top with a spoonful of the compote.

The compote can be refrigerated (don't remove the spices) for up to a week. Bring to room temperature or rewarm before serving.

real hot fudge sundaes

I used to make this sauce in a five-gallon bucket when I was pastry chef at Chicago's famous Pump Room restaurant. We served "The World's Smallest Hot Fudge Sundae" (one of my friend and partner Rich Melman's many brilliant ideas) and it was so popular that even though each mini-sundae used only two tablespoons of sauce, I had to make a huge batch every other day!

For a more elegant occasion, simply pour the chocolate sauce over the vanilla ice cream at the table, leaving off the whipped cream and nuts. This is a good quick trick for entertaining: Homemade sauce and real whipped cream transform store-bought ice cream into a special dessert.

MAKES 4 TO 6 SERVINGS

1 cup sugar

4 cups (1 quart) heavy cream

1/4 cup light corn syrup, such as Karo

4 ounces best-quality unsweetened chocolate, chopped (see page 15)

4 tablespoons (1/2 stick) salted butter

1 tablespoon pure vanilla extract

1 pint vanilla ice cream, such as Ben & Jerry's World's Greatest Vanilla

Chopped walnuts or peanuts, for sprinkling

1. Combine the sugar, 3 cups of the cream, the corn syrup, chocolate, and butter in a saucepan and bring to a boil. Reduce the heat to a very slow simmer and continue cooking, stirring often, until the mixture looks curdled (this is a sign that the cocoa butter and butterfat are separating from the other ingredients), at least 20 to 30 minutes. Remove from the heat, whisk in the vanilla, and blend the mixture with a hand blender (or whisk it vigorously) to smooth it out. The sauce should be thick, smooth, and glossy.*

2. Just before serving, reheat the sauce in a microwave or in the top of a double boiler set over simmering water and whisk until smooth. Whip the remaining 1 cup cold heavy cream into soft peaks. Place 2 or 3 scoops of ice cream in each serving dish, pour the hot fudge sauce over, and top with whipped cream and chopped nuts. You will have plenty of sauce left over.

* *The sauce can be made and refrigerated up to 2 weeks in advance.*

quicker pear and ginger
scones

When I looked at my favorite scone recipe to see if it could be made even easier, I found it needed just a tiny tweak. The traditional method calls for rolling out the dough on a floured surface, then cutting it into wedges—but I find that simply scooping rough lumps of dough out of the bowl with an ice-cream scoop works just as well! I love a bumpy, crusty scone.

If you like a powerful ginger flavor and even more chewiness, add some minced crystallized ginger. You can really use any dried fruit and any warm spice, such as cinnamon.

MAKES 12 LARGE SCONES

3³⁄₄ cups all-purpose flour
¹⁄₄ teaspoon salt
¹⁄₄ cup sugar
3 tablespoons baking powder
1 teaspoon ground ginger

8 tablespoons (1 stick) cold
    unsalted butter
1¹⁄₄ cups milk
1¹⁄₂ cups dried pear pieces (use
    scissors to cut into pieces the
    size of raisins)

1. Preheat the oven to 375 degrees. Set the oven rack in the top half of the oven.

2. In a mixer fitted with a paddle attachment (or using a hand mixer), mix the flour, salt, sugar, baking powder, and ginger at low speed. Cut the butter into small pieces. With the mixer running, add the butter and mix until coarse and sandy. You should still see small lumps of butter.✳

3. Add the milk and mix until almost combined, then add the dried pear chunks and mix just to distribute them evenly through the dough. Mix just until smooth and all the ingredients are incorporated.

4. Use a large ice-cream scoop to scoop the dough onto an ungreased sheet pan, leaving 1¹⁄₂ inches between the scones. Bake until light golden brown, 18 to 20 minutes. Serve warm.

✳ *This mixture can be refrigerated overnight. Proceed with the recipe the next day, and serve warm, right after they are made, for the best flavor. Scones do not age gracefully!*

aunt greta's
walnut meringues

This is one of my beloved aunt's tried-and-true recipes to serve with tea. I love heirloom recipes because they bring the person who gave you the recipe right into the kitchen with you. The combination of cinnamon and nuts makes a comforting pick-me-up on a cold afternoon, and the cookies are very light.

Nuts are one of the handiest ingredients for quick desserts from the pantry. Hazelnuts, pecans, and pine nuts would also work well if you happen to have them on hand.

MAKES 20 TO 25 COOKIES

1 large egg white
½ cup sugar
1 teaspoon cinnamon

Pinch of salt
1 cup walnut pieces, toasted
    (page 17) and cooled

1. Heat the oven to 300 degrees. Line a sheet pan with nonstick baking mats or parchment paper, or use a heavyweight nonstick sheet pan. Whip the egg white in a mixer fitted with a whisk attachment until almost stiff. Add the sugar, cinnamon, and salt and continue whipping until stiff. Fold in the walnuts with a rubber scraper.

2. Drop the mixture by ½ teaspoonfuls onto the sheet pan, leaving an inch between them (they will spread), and bake for 35 to 40 minutes, until crisp and faintly browned on the outside. Let cool and remove from the pan. Store in an airtight container.✳

✳ *As long as the weather is not too humid, the meringues will keep for 3 to 4 days. In high humidity, make and eat the meringues the same day.*

cornmeal–walnut
shortbread coins

SEE PHOTOGRAPH PAGE 25

Somewhere between a cookie and a rich, buttery cracker, these are great with cheese and a glass of port, or alongside a fruit dessert. I also love them plain with a cup of tea or with a dab of Plum Jam (page 125). Toasty flavor from the butter, cornmeal, and walnuts makes them special, and they have a nice pale golden color. You can keep the dough frozen in logs and slice and bake the logs one at a time, as you need the cookies, making this a very convenient recipe to keep on hand.

Adding a little cornmeal to a cookie dough or cake batter is one of my favorite quick tricks for adding color, texture, and flavor to simple desserts.

MAKES ABOUT 80 COOKIES

10 tablespoons (1¼ sticks) unsalted butter, slightly softened
½ cup confectioners' sugar
1 teaspoon pure vanilla extract
2 cups all-purpose flour

6 tablespoons yellow cornmeal or polenta, plus extra for coating
Heaping ½ teaspoon salt
½ cup toasted chopped walnuts (page 17)

1. In a mixer fitted with the paddle attachment, cream the butter until smooth. Mix in the confectioners' sugar. Mix in the vanilla. Add the remaining ingredients and mix until blended. Spread some cornmeal out on a plate or on a clean work surface. Divide the dough in half and roll into logs 1½ inches in diameter, then roll the logs in cornmeal to coat them. Wrap each log in plastic wrap and refrigerate for at least one hour or overnight.＊

2. When ready to bake, heat the oven to 300 degrees. Butter a sheet pan or line it with parchment paper or a baking mat (or use a heavyweight nonstick sheet pan). Slice each log into coins (about ⅛ to ¼ inch thick) and arrange on the pan; they won't spread much, so you can place them close together. Bake the cookies for 15 to 20 minutes (they will still be blond in color, not browned). Let cool on the pans. Store in an airtight container.＊＊

＊ *The plastic-wrapped logs of dough can be kept frozen for up to 2 weeks.*
＊＊ *Once the cookies are baked, serve them within 3 days.*

cherry clafouti

Clafouti is delicious, comforting, and such a handy dessert to know. It works with almost any fruit—and all the batter ingredients are always likely to be on hand in your kitchen. This rustic French dessert is really just a tender pancake batter poured over fresh or (in the case of hard fruit like apples or pears) lightly cooked fruit. Classic black cherry makes my favorite clafouti, but raspberries, blueberries, or blackberries will work just as well.

MAKES 6 TO 8 SERVINGS

1 cup milk

3 large eggs

1 cup all-purpose flour

⅓ cup sugar

2 cups fresh or 1 (10-ounce) bag frozen pitted black or other ripe, sweet cherries

Confectioners' sugar, for sprinkling

1. In a saucepan, bring the milk to a boil, then immediately turn off the heat. Whisk the eggs in a medium bowl. Gradually whisk in the flour, then the sugar, and finally the hot milk, mixing thoroughly until smooth. If possible, set aside at room temperature for at least 2 hours (letting it stand makes a more tender batter). *

2. When ready to bake, heat the oven to 325 degrees and butter a 9-inch round cake pan. Stir the batter well, then strain into the pan through a sieve, to remove any lumps. Dot the surface evenly with the cherries and bake for 35 to 40 minutes, until puffed and light golden brown. Sprinkle with confectioners' sugar and serve warm, cut into wedges.

If not baking within 2 hours, you can keep the batter refrigerated for up to 1 day. If you're baking the batter right out of the refrigerator, you may need to add 5 to 10 minutes to the baking time.

strawberry-rhubarb slump

A slump is in the family of fruit desserts with dough on top, like cobblers and grunts. This is like a fluffy steamed dumpling over fruit compote, which "slumps" when you put it on the plate. Tart rhubarb and sweet berries make a perfect combination, and the natural pectin in rhubarb makes the filling thick and jammy.

This hearty dessert reminds me of my mom's favorite winter lunch: tomato soup with dumplings. She'd slip the batter off a large spoon into the simmering red bath of soup, and in a few minutes we would have a treasure hunt to find the dumplings at the bottom of the saucepan.

MAKES 4 TO 6 SERVINGS

2 cups strawberries, trimmed
   and cut into large pieces
2 cups rhubarb, fresh or frozen,
   cut into 1-inch pieces
1/2 cup plus 2 tablespoons sugar
1 cup all-purpose flour, sifted
   after measuring

2 teaspoons baking powder
1/4 teaspoon salt
1/2 cup milk
1/4 teaspoon freshly grated
   lemon zest
Heavy cream or vanilla ice
   cream (optional)

1. Combine the strawberries, rhubarb, 1/2 cup sugar, and 1/2 cup water in a deep, heavy skillet with a lid. Bring to a simmer over medium heat. Simmer gently for about 10 minutes.

2. Meanwhile, in a bowl, stir together the remaining 2 tablespoons sugar, the flour, baking powder, and salt.*

3. Add the milk and zest to the dry ingredients and quickly mix into a batter. Drop the batter by spoonfuls onto the surface of the simmering fruit. Cook, uncovered, for 10 minutes, then cover and cook for another 10 minutes. Serve in shallow bowls, topped with heavy cream or ice cream if desired.

* *The fruit can be cooked and the dry ingredients can be mixed together up to 4 hours in advance. Once cooked, the slump should be served as soon as possible.*

pumpkin pots

I developed this recipe as a simple substitute for pumpkin pie, and it really works! I like not having to worry about the crust getting soggy, the way you do with pumpkin pie; instead, I just serve the pumpkin mousse with crisp cookies like Snickerdoodles (page 151) or Langues-de-Chat (page 76) on the side. It's custardy and smooth, but easier than custard because you can simply bake it in ramekins resting in a roasting pan, with no water bath needed!

MAKES 8 SERVINGS

1 (15-ounce) can unsweetened pumpkin purée (not flavored pumpkin pie filling)
3 large eggs
$\frac{1}{2}$ cup granulated sugar
$\frac{1}{2}$ cup light brown sugar, packed

$1\frac{3}{4}$ teaspoons pumpkin pie spice or 1 teaspoon cinnamon, $\frac{1}{2}$ teaspoon cloves, and $\frac{1}{4}$ teaspoon nutmeg
$\frac{1}{2}$ teaspoon salt
$\frac{1}{2}$ cup whole milk
$\frac{1}{2}$ cup heavy cream

1. Preheat the oven to 350 degrees.

2. With a whisk (or using a mixer), blend the pumpkin purée and eggs together very well. Add the sugars and mix. Add the remaining ingredients and mix until blended and smooth.*

3. Divide the mixture evenly among 8 ovenproof cups or ramekins (see page 21). Place the ramekins in a roasting pan or on a sheet pan. Bake until set and lightly browned on the top, 35 to 40 minutes. (A knife inserted into the center should come out almost completely clean.)

4. Let cool slightly and serve warm, or refrigerate and serve chilled.**

* The pumpkin mixture can be refrigerated for up to 2 days.

** If you're baking the pots right out of the refrigerator, you may need to add 5 to 10 minutes to the baking time. The baked pots can be refrigerated for up to 3 days.

ricotta–sweet potato beignets

I first tasted sheep's-milk ricotta cheese at the Old Chatham Sheepherding Company, a delightful dairy farm in upstate New York where the milk comes from sheep (instead of cows) and the shepherds are llamas (instead of dogs). Sheep's milk is richer, higher in calcium, and sweeter than cow's or goat's milk, and it makes wonderful cheese. These beignets have a wonderful crisp gold-brown crust and tender insides, like a dessert version of hush puppies.

You can use any good-quality ricotta for this recipe, or even a mild fresh goat cheese. It adds moisture and a little richness to the dough, binding the ingredients together without making it wet.

MAKES ABOUT 15 BEIGNETS

1 cup mashed cooked sweet potato

$\frac{1}{2}$ cup fresh ricotta cheese, preferably sheep's milk (see above)

$\frac{1}{2}$ cup all-purpose flour

1 large egg white

$\frac{1}{4}$ cup sugar

Pinch of salt

$\frac{3}{4}$ teaspoon baking powder

$\frac{1}{4}$ teaspoon pure vanilla extract

Vegetable oil, for frying

Confectioners' sugar, for sprinkling

1. Combine all the ingredients in a mixer fitted with a paddle attachment and mix until smooth. Roll into $1\frac{1}{2}$-inch balls (the size of a walnut) and set aside on a plate. Refrigerate until ready to cook.*

2. Just before serving, heat 2 to 3 inches of oil in a deep, heavy pot fitted with a deep-frying thermometer to 365 degrees. Working in batches to avoid crowding the pot, fry the balls until golden brown all over, moving them around in the oil to make sure they cook and brown evenly. Remove from the oil and drain on paper towels or brown paper. Repeat with remaining beignets, making sure to let the oil return to 365 degrees between batches. Dust the beignets with confectioners' sugar and serve warm.

* The dough balls can be refrigerated for up to 1 day before cooking.

roasted apricots
with bay leaf and broiled sugar brioche

The book you are reading grew from the seed of this one recipe. Roasting fruit in the oven with a little sugar and butter is so easy and quick, and such an obvious way to make dessert, that I can't believe I didn't think of it years ago! There are several roasted-fruit recipes in this chapter; I hope they will lead you to come up with new desserts of your own, because any stone fruit works really well. Apricots are perfect candidates for roasting; the high heat brings out both the sweetness and the tartness of the fruit.

I fell in love with bay leaves when I lived in the English countryside; the big, glossy bushes (they call them laurel) are everywhere, grown for their good looks rather than for flavoring. Bay is a strong, pungent herb, like rosemary: The fresh and dried versions are pretty much the same for cooking purposes.

For the fruit
2 tablespoons unsalted butter
2 tablespoons light brown sugar
1 bay leaf, fresh or dried,
    broken in 4 pieces
¼ cup whole blanched or
    peeled almonds, toasted
    (see page 17)
6 apricots, halved and pitted

For the toast
3 tablespoons unsalted butter, at
    room temperature
3 tablespoons granulated sugar
6 slices of brioche or challah

Vanilla ice cream, for serving
    (optional)

1. Heat the oven to 400 degrees.

2. Combine the butter, brown sugar, bay leaf, and almonds in a small (about 8 × 8-inch square) baking dish. Bake for 5 minutes, until the butter is melted. Remove from the oven and stir to combine the ingredients. Add the apricots and gently toss to coat with the butter mixture.*

3. Turn the apricots cut side down and bake until they begin to feel tender, 5 to 8 minutes. Set aside in the baking dish.

4. Meanwhile, start the toast: In a small bowl, mash the butter and sugar together. Lightly toast the bread in the toaster, then use the butter mixture to thickly butter the bread on one side, covering the entire surface including the crusts (this will protect them from burning).

5. When ready to serve, preheat the broiler to high (or use your toaster oven). Broil the slices (not too close to the heat) until toasted and caramelized, 1 to 2 minutes. Cut in half diagonally. To serve, place two apricot halves, cut side up, in each bowl. If using ice cream, scoop it next to the fruit. Drizzle the pan juices over and sprinkle the almonds on the top. Tuck 2 pieces of toast into the bowl and serve.

You can prepare the apricots up to this point 1 day ahead and refrigerate, covered. Do the baking and broiling at the last minute, so that the apricots will be warm. If you're baking the apricots straight out of the fridge, add 3 minutes to the cooking time.

roasted peaches
with thyme and ricotta

This luxurious dessert is all about enhancing the natural voluptuousness of ripe peaches. Some summers I am lucky enough to get big, juicy peaches from Michigan all season long, and each bushel is better than the last one.

The vanilla, lemon, and honey in the recipe are all flavors that you can taste in a really ripe peach. You may be surprised to see herbs from the savory side of the kitchen—pepper and thyme—here as well. They add an herbal spiciness that makes you notice the sweet fruitiness of the peach even more, the same way an old, complex wine can bring out the flavor of fruit. This dessert is amazing with a glass of sweet dessert wine such as Beaumes de Venise or Beerenauslese.

MAKES 6 SERVINGS

1 tablespoon unsalted butter
1/2 vanilla bean, split lengthwise
Strips of fresh lemon peel (avoid the white pith as much as possible), about 10 inches total (from 1 or 2 lemons)
1 sprig of fresh thyme, plus extra for garnish

8 black peppercorns
3 to 6 ripe peaches (depending on size), halved lengthwise and pitted
2 tablespoons honey
1/4 cup fresh ricotta cheese

1. Heat the oven to 400 degrees. Place the butter in a baking pan and put it in the oven to melt. When the butter is melted, use the tip of a sharp knife to scrape the insides of the vanilla bean into the pan, reserving the outside pod. Strip the leaves off the thyme sprig. Sprinkle the thyme leaves, lemon peel, and peppercorns into the pan. Place the peaches, cut side down, in the pan. Drizzle with honey and lay the vanilla pod on top of the peaches.*

2. Bake until the peaches are slightly slumped and feel a little soft, about 15 minutes. Let cool in the pan to room temperature.

3. To serve, turn the peaches over and arrange in a serving dish. Strain the pan juices to make a little sauce for drizzling. Spoon the ricotta into the cavity of each peach. Drizzle with sauce, garnish with thyme sprigs, and serve.

✳ *The dish can be assembled up to this point and refrigerated, covered, overnight. If baking the peaches right out of the refrigerator, add about 3 minutes to the cooking time.*

strawberries with white balsamic and creamy yogurt

I serve this in the summer when Wisconsin strawberries are at their peak. It's so refreshing and is the best version of strawberries and cream I've ever had. Thick, creamy Mediterranean yogurt is available in more and more American supermarkets, and it really has a fabulously different effect from the yogurt we're used to. It's sometimes labeled "Greek yogurt" or "Mediterranean yogurt," and it has a fresh, sweet flavor. You can make any yogurt thicker by draining it in the refrigerator for a few hours, in a strainer lined with cheesecloth or a coffee filter.

A touch of balsamic vinegar is a spectacular Italian quick trick for bringing out the flavor of ripe strawberries: I use white balsamic, made from green grapes instead of red, because the flavor is less tannic and the berries stay brighter-looking. But you can use regular balsamic vinegar, as long as it has a good balance of sweetness and acid; taste as you add.

MAKES 4 TO 6 SERVINGS

1 pint (2 cups) ripe strawberries, green tops removed, berries cut into large chunks

2 tablespoons sugar

2 tablespoons to ¼ cup balsamic vinegar, preferably white (see above)

1 teaspoon chervil, tarragon, or mint leaves

1 cup thick yogurt (see above) or any good-quality whole-milk yogurt

In a nonreactive bowl, toss the berries with the sugar, half of the vinegar, and the chervil (if using tarragon or mint, cut the leaves into fine strips or shreds before adding). Refrigerate for at least 2 hours.* When ready to serve, taste for sugar and vinegar and adjust the flavorings. Place a large spoonful of the berries in each serving bowl. Spoon a large dollop of yogurt next to the berries. Drizzle a little of the juice from the bottom of the bowl over each dessert.

The berries can be refrigerated for up to 12 hours.

zabaglione with fresh berries

Elegant and easy, easy, easy. Now that we can get good berries all year round, I recommend this dessert as the ending of a grown-up dinner party—just ripe berries topped with a frothy, warm, custardy sauce. There's something about cooking up desserts *a là minute*, at the last minute, that just makes people melt.

Zabaglione is sometimes served for breakfast in Italy, as it's made mostly from eggs. Marsala, a sweet wine from Sicily, is the traditional choice for zabaglione, but you could also use Madeira or a light-colored tawny port.

MAKES 4 SERVINGS

1 cup raspberries
1 cup blackberries or blueberries
8 egg yolks
$\frac{1}{2}$ cup sugar
1 cup Marsala wine (see above)

1. Gently mix the berries together and divide them among 4 serving dishes (I like to use martini glasses or other wide-mouth stemmed glasses).

2. Bring an inch of water to a simmer in a medium or large saucepan. Whisk the yolks and sugar together in a bowl, preferably copper or metal. Set the pan over the simmering (not boiling) water, and continue to whisk the mixture constantly. As it cooks, it will turn thick and lighten to a pale yellow. When you can see that it's beginning to thicken, start gradually whisking in the wine. Continue to cook until very light and fluffy, 4 to 6 minutes total. Pour the hot zabaglione over the berries and serve immediately.*

* Serve this fast dessert as soon as it is made.

{banana
bisque

A simply sumptuous brew of bananas and cream, scented with the sweet perfume of vanilla and edged with the bitterness of coffee. This warm, luxurious dessert was inspired by my love for the melted ice cream left in the bowl at the end of a banana split; I always find myself spooning it up from the bowl long after the chill is gone. Each mouthful is lush and satisfying.

MAKES 4 TO 6 SERVINGS

$1^{1}/_{2}$ **cups heavy cream**
4 tablespoons ($^{1}/_{2}$ stick) unsalted butter
$^{1}/_{4}$ **cup sugar**
Pinch of salt

$^{1}/_{4}$ **vanilla bean, split lengthwise**
2 ripe bananas
Espresso Granita (page 107) or coffee ice cream for serving (optional)

1. Combine the cream, butter, sugar, salt, and vanilla bean in a saucepan and bring to a boil. Remove from the heat and stir to dissolve the sugar. Remove the vanilla bean.✳

2. When ready to serve, heat the bisque through over medium heat. Peel and slice the bananas and add them to the liquid. Stir gently and turn off the heat.

3. Scoop the granita or ice cream into shallow serving bowls and ladle the hot bisque and bananas around the granita. Serve immediately.

✳ *The recipe can be made up to this point and kept refrigerated up to 3 days in advance.*

peach and blueberry floats

Summer in a glass. This is really refreshing, simple, and delicious. The only cooking you do involves making a simple purée of berries. We serve tiny floats with little scoops of ice cream as a treat before the full dessert course at Tru, using whatever summer fruits and berries are ripest that day. But the float makes a great dessert on its own or with cookies.

Floats are a favorite quick trick of mine for a casual dessert: They are retro, charming, delicious, and light after a big meal. And *so* easy to put together: A float can be as simple as root beer and vanilla ice cream. If I do say so myself, my own Gale's Root Beer makes the best floats I've ever tasted.

MAKES 6 SERVINGS

1 cup (1/2 pint) blueberries
1/4 cup sugar
1 large peach
Peach ice cream, or another
    homemade or store-bought
    ice cream of your choice

Sparkling water
Straws, elbow if possible

1. Set about 18 blueberries aside and place the remainder in a saucepan with the sugar and 2 tablespoons of water. Bring to a boil, then reduce the heat and simmer for 3 minutes. Mash the cooked berries in the pan with a rubber scraper and pass the blueberry purée through a strainer to remove the skins. Fold the whole berries into the purée and refrigerate until ready to serve.✳

2. When ready to serve, cut half of the peach into small cubes and the other half into 6 wedges. Set out 6 small glasses (4 to 6 ounces each) and cut down the straws to 1 inch above the height of the glasses. In each glass, place a spoonful of the blueberry mixture, a few cubes of fresh peach, and a small scoop of ice cream. Slowly fill the glasses with sparkling water. Slip one peach wedge onto the rim of each glass and stick in a straw. Serve immediately.

✳ *The blueberry mixture can be kept refrigerated for up to 5 days.*

orange panna cotta

Panna cotta, a simple mixture of cream and gelatin, is a busy cook's best friend. It gives you the luscious, trembling texture of a cool custard, without any of the painstaking cooking and stirring. Really, it's more like making Jell-O. All you do is mix and chill—but since you're using fresh ingredients, the taste is all homemade. This particular combination of orange and vanilla flavors is my homage to the Creamsicle.

MAKES 6 TO 8 SERVINGS

1 tablespoon unflavored dry gelatin

4 cups heavy cream, or 2 cups cream and 2 cups milk or buttermilk

1/2 vanilla bean, split lengthwise

6 wide strips of freshly peeled orange zest (orange part only)

3/4 cup sugar

A small block of milk chocolate, for garnish (optional)

1. Pour 3 tablespoons of cool water into a small bowl. Sprinkle the gelatin over the water a little bit at a time and let soak for about 10 minutes (do not stir).

2. Meanwhile, heat the cream, vanilla bean, orange zest, and sugar to a simmer in a medium saucepan over medium heat, stirring occasionally to dissolve the sugar. As soon as it simmers, turn off the heat and add the gelatin mixture, stirring to dissolve the gelatin. If the gelatin doesn't completely dissolve in 3 minutes, return the mixture to the heat and warm gently until dissolved.

3. Strain the mixture into a pitcher to remove the vanilla bean and orange rind. Pour the mixture into 6 to 8 ramekins or dessert cups (see page 21), or into one larger dish. Chill, uncovered, for at least 3 hours.*

4. To unmold, dip the bottoms of the cups in hot water for 10 seconds, then shake the panna cottas out onto dessert plates (or, simply serve in the cups or by big spoonfuls). If they don't come right out, run a knife around the edges to break the suction and try again. Using a vegetable peeler and a block of chocolate, shave chocolate curls onto the tops of each serving. Serve cold.

* *Covered and refrigerated, the panna cotta will keep for up to 3 days.*

grilled pecorino
with fresh figs and honey

SEE PHOTOGRAPH PAGE 9

I first tasted grilled Pecorino in San Gimignano, a small walled village in the hills of Tuscany where no cars are allowed. I spent the morning building up an appetite by walking up and down the steep streets, then had this combination for lunch, with red wine, of course! Sometimes the cheese is served with the famous local *panforte*, a dried fruit, honey, and nut cake, but simply serving it with dried fruit and nuts is just as tasty. It makes a perfect dessert and cheese course all in one. It may seem odd to cook plain cheese in a frying pan, but don't worry: The Pecorino Romano is firm enough to brown on the outside and stay intact.

In Italy, the pistachio nuts from Sicily, with its rich volcanic soil, are the most prized. But any fresh ones will do.

MAKES 6 SERVINGS

½ **pound Pecorino Romano cheese, in one piece**

2 **tablespoons sugar**

6 **fresh figs, halved lengthwise**

⅓ **cup shelled pistachio nuts (not dyed), coarsely chopped**

¼ **cup honey**

1. Using a heavy, sharp knife, cut the cheese into 6 slices, each about ¼ inch thick. Spread the sugar out on a plate and dip the cut faces of the figs in it, just to coat. Set aside.

2. Heat a large, nonstick skillet over medium-high heat until the surface is very hot. Add the cheese and figs (cut faces down) and cook until the cheese is browned on the bottom. Turn off the heat and let cool slightly, just until the cheese is firm enough to move.

3. Serve immediately: Place a piece of cheese on a dessert plate, tuck 2 fig halves next to it, and sprinkle on a tablespoon of pistachios. Lightly drizzle the surface of the cheese with honey.

dulce de leche
on toasted pound cake

Lovers of crème caramel (page 132) must try this ridiculously simple recipe for *dulce de leche*, the luscious golden "milk candy" that is popular all over Latin America and the Caribbean. *Dulce de leche* is made by caramelizing the natural sugars in condensed milk, which can be done right in the can! It's a very safe way to make caramel, and kids (and grown-ups) find it fascinating.

The result is a smooth, creamy, *easy* caramel sauce. To make a thicker caramel filling for a cake or pastry, simmer the can for 1½ hours.

MAKES 8 TO 12 SERVINGS

1 (14-ounce) can sweetened condensed milk
1 homemade or good-quality store-bought
    pound cake
1 pint chocolate or vanilla ice cream

1. Remove the label from the can (do not open or puncture it). Stand the can up in a saucepan and cover it with water. Bring the water to a gentle simmer and simmer for 1 hour, refilling the pan with hot water as needed to keep the can covered. Let cool, then open the can and pour into a serving pitcher. The milk will be tan in color and look like smooth, creamy caramel sauce.*

2. Just before serving, slice the pound cake and toast the slices lightly in the toaster. If necessary, warm the dulce de leche in the microwave to make it more pourable. Place each slice of cake on a serving plate, add a scoop of ice cream, and pour the dulce de leche over the top.

* *The dulce de leche can be covered and kept refrigerated for at least 1 week.*

roasted pineapple skewers

At summer cookouts, I take advantage of the natural sweetness in a ripe pineapple by throwing it on the grill. High heat can caramelize all those sugars, giving the fruit a wonderful burnt-sugar edge. To pick out a ripe pineapple, smell the bottom; it should smell fragrant and sweet. Also, look at the color of the skin: The more yellow and less green you see, the riper the fruit. A pineapple will continue to ripen after it's picked, so you can buy one that is still a bit green and ripen it in a sunny spot in your kitchen.

MAKES 8 TO 12 SERVINGS

1 ripe fresh pineapple, peeled or unpeeled (I use the leaves to garnish the dish, but it's optional)
2 tablespoons dark rum (optional)
1/2 cup pure maple syrup
1/2 cup large blueberries
2 pints vanilla ice cream
Thin wooden skewers

1. To peel the pineapple, cut off the top. Reserve the best-looking leaves for decoration by placing them in a bowl of cold water (you'll want 2 leaves per serving). Cut off the bottom. Use a large, sharp knife to cut off the peel from top to bottom, following the contours of the fruit. Cut out any eyes. Cut the pineapple in half from top to bottom, then cut each half in half lengthwise. Cut out the cores.

2. Cut the pineapple into 1½-inch chunks. If you're using the rum, stir it together with the maple syrup. Toss the pineapple chunks in the maple syrup and then thread them, alternating with the blueberries, onto the wooden skewers.*

3. Just before grilling, brush the fruit one more time with maple syrup. Fire up your grill and place the skewers on to cook them, turning occasionally. Cook until softened and glazed, about 5 minutes total. To serve, scoop the ice cream into bowls. Stick 2 pineapple leaves at the back of each bowl (make them stand up like rabbit ears) and rest a skewer or two across the rim of the bowl. If desired, pour any remaining maple syrup over the top.

* *The pineapple can be mixed with the maple syrup and even threaded onto the skewers up to a day in advance. Keep the skewers in a shallow dish where they can marinate in the syrup until you cook them.*

30-minute recipes

chocolate–croissant
bread pudding

Using croissants as the bread in bread pudding is even better than you might imagine: Not only is the croissant incredibly buttery, but the chocolate custard seeps right in between all those layers of flaky pastry.

Cooking with day-old bread (and croissants) is a handy and thrifty quick trick. Bread that is starting to dry out is more absorbent than fresh, so it's always the best choice for bread puddings that are moist but firm. Fresh bread tends to fall apart and turn to mush.

MAKES 6 TO 8 SERVINGS

4 to 6 croissants, preferably 1 or
　　2 days old (see above)
2 cups half-and-half
2 cups heavy cream
4 ounces semisweet or bitter-
　　sweet chocolate, chopped

Pinch of salt
6 eggs
1 cup sugar
Vanilla ice cream, for serving
　　(optional)

1. Cut the croissants into 1-inch cubes. You should have about 3½ cups. Place the cubes in a medium-size baking dish.

2. In a saucepan, heat the half-and-half and cream over medium-high heat, stirring occasionally to make sure the mixture doesn't burn or stick to the bottom of the pan. When the cream mixture reaches a fast simmer (do not let it boil), turn off the heat. Add the chocolate and salt and whisk until melted.

3. In a large mixing bowl, whisk the eggs and sugar together. Whisking constantly, gradually add the hot chocolate–cream mixture. Strain the mixture over the croissant pieces and toss lightly. Refrigerate until the mixture is absorbed, at least 15 minutes. As it soaks, fold the mixture a few times to ensure even soaking.*

4. When ready to bake, heat the oven to 350 degrees and prepare a hot-water bath (see page 23). Bake until the pudding is set in the center, 40 to 45 minutes. Serve warm, with a scoop of vanilla ice cream on each serving, if desired.

The mixture can be covered at this point and refrigerated for up to 1 day. If baking the pudding straight from the fridge, add 5 to 10 minutes to the baking time.

velvety cocoa cake

Since cocoa is the essence of chocolate flavor—it's the pure, unsweetened meat of the cocoa bean, with all the cocoa butter removed—it makes a deeper, darker chocolate cake than melted chocolate does but one that is feather-light.

If you like dark-roast coffee, try making this cake with the dark-roast cocoa called "black cocoa." Black cocoa is what gives Oreo cookies their distinctive color and flavor; you can buy it from the King Arthur Flour Company's *Baker's Catalogue* (800-827-6836).

MAKES 1 CAKE

12 tablespoons (1$\frac{1}{2}$ sticks) unsalted
    butter, slightly softened
1$\frac{3}{4}$ cups granulated sugar
2 large eggs
1 teaspoon pure vanilla extract
$\frac{1}{2}$ cup best-quality cocoa powder

2$\frac{1}{4}$ cups sifted cake flour
1$\frac{1}{4}$ teaspoons baking soda
$\frac{3}{4}$ teaspoon salt

Confectioners' sugar, for garnish
    (optional)

1. Heat the oven to 350 degrees. Butter and flour a Bundt pan or tube pan (you can use a mixture of cocoa and flour to prevent white spots on the cake). For the best results, do this even if you're using a nonstick pan.

2. In a mixer fitted with a whisk attachment, or using a hand mixer, cream the butter until light and fluffy. Mix in the granulated sugar. One at a time, mix in the eggs, then the vanilla, scraping down the mixing bowl occasionally.

3. Fill a measuring cup with 1$\frac{1}{4}$ cups of very cold water. In a separate bowl, sift together the cocoa powder, cake flour, baking soda, and salt. Mix about a third of the dry ingredients into the batter, then a third of the water. Repeat with the remaining ingredients, mixing after each addition. Pour the batter into the prepared pan.

4. Bake in the top half of the oven until springy and dry in the center, 40 to 45 minutes. Let cool completely in the pan on a rack, then carefully turn the cake out. Just before serving, sift confectioners' sugar over the top.*

This cake tastes best the day after it's made and keeps up to 5 days.

chocolate angel food cake with espresso glaze

This cake is a happy compromise between good and wicked. It has the light, fluffy texture (and low fat content) of an angel food cake, with all the powerful chocolate flavor of a devil's food cake. The intense espresso glaze really makes it satisfying.

Tube pans (the ones with a hole in the middle and straight, smooth sides) are used for angel food cakes to allow the delicate batter to cook quickly and evenly. Cooling the cake upside down prevents it from deflating as it cools. In fact, many tube pans are made with little legs on the top to hold the pan up when turned upside down. I often see them at tag sales, a wonderful source for perfectly good, lightly used cookware.

MAKES 10 TO 12 SERVINGS

For the cake
¾ cup granulated sugar
5 tablespoons best-quality cocoa powder, such as Valrhona or Droste
¾ cup sifted cake flour
1¾ cups egg whites (from about 12 large eggs)
¾ teaspoon salt
1½ teaspoons cream of tartar
1 teaspoon pure vanilla extract

For the glaze (optional)
3 tablespoons brewed espresso or strong coffee
1¼ cups confectioners' sugar

1. Heat the oven to 400 degrees.

2. Combine ½ cup of the granulated sugar with the cocoa and the flour and sift together 3 times (this is to lighten the mixture).

3. In a clean, dry bowl, whip the egg whites and salt until foamy. Add the cream of tartar and whip until soft peaks form. Add the remaining ¼ cup granulated sugar and whip just until stiff but not dry. The peaks should be slightly glossy. By hand, fold in the vanilla. Gradually fold in the dry ingredients.

4. Spoon the batter into an ungreased tube pan and smooth the top. Bake for 35 minutes, or until dry and springy. To cool, turn the pan upside down and hang it around the neck of a bottle. After the cake has cooled completely, run a butter knife around the walls of the pan to cut off the outside layer of crumb and leave it stuck to the pan. Turn the cake out and brush off any loose crumbs. If using, make the glaze by whisking the coffee and confectioners' sugar together. Drizzle the glaze over the top of the cake, letting it run down the sides. Let it set for at least 1 hour before serving.*

Like all angel food cakes, this one is best mixed, baked, and served on the same day.

chocolate-coconut macaroon pies

The "dough" for coconut macaroons is so easy to make—just sugar, egg whites, and coconut—that I was tempted to see what else it could do. It's easier to work with than a pastry dough because there is no need to roll it out, it stays wherever you press it, and it holds its shape well after baking. These little cups of toasted coconut, full of creamy dark chocolate, are like chocolate-dipped macaroons in reverse: lots of chocolate and a little coconut. I love the flavors together.

MAKES 24

Heaping ³⁄₄ cup sugar
Scant ¹⁄₂ cup egg whites (from about
    3 large eggs)
³⁄₄ pound (scant 2¹⁄₂ cups) sweetened
    flaked coconut, such as Baker's

8 ounces semisweet chocolate,
    chopped (see page 15)
¹⁄₂ cup heavy cream
A few toasted almonds (see page 17),
    chopped

1. Heat the oven to 350 degrees.

2. Mix the sugar, egg whites, and coconut together. Put a spoonful into each of 24 nonstick mini-muffin cups or individual tart molds. Press the "dough" into the molds to make little cups, with sides and a well for holding the chocolate filling. Bake until golden, 12 to 15 minutes. Let cool completely in the pans, then gently remove.* (You may need to run a plastic knife around the rim of the cups to loosen them.)

3. To make the filling, place the chocolate in a bowl. Heat the cream in a small sauce-pan just until boiling, then pour it over the chocolate and let it sit for 1 minute. Whisk gently to melt the chocolate completely. Keep whisking until smooth and glossy.

4. Fill the tarts by pouring in the warm chocolate filling. Sprinkle a few pieces of chopped almond in the center of each tart while they're still warm. Let them set at room temperature for at least 1 hour before serving, and serve them the same day they are made.

The coconut shells can be baked up to 2 days in advance and kept at room temperature in an airtight container. The chocolate ganache can be refrigerated for up to 5 days; rewarm it in the microwave or in a bowl set over simmering water until it is pourable.

chewy chocolate chip–espresso cookies

Warm cookies after dinner are a really special dessert. Baking the cookies straight from the freezer helps ensure a moist, fudgy center with a shiny, crackly top. It also means that you can make the cookie dough well in advance and just bake the cookies at the very last minute—a great quick trick that works with most cookies! If you bake them without freezing first, reduce the baking time to 5 minutes. (These cookies are pictured on page 143.)

MAKES ABOUT 30 COOKIES

1¾ cups plus ¾ cup semisweet
    chocolate chips
4 tablespoons (½ stick) unsalted butter
¼ cup all-purpose flour
¼ teaspoon baking powder

¼ teaspoon salt
2 large eggs
¾ cup sugar
1 teaspoon ground espresso or other
    finely ground dark-roast coffee beans

1. Melt the 1¾ cups chocolate chips and the butter together in a double boiler or a bowl set over simmering water. Meanwhile, mix together the flour, baking powder, and salt.

2. In a mixer fitted with a whisk attachment, mix the eggs and sugar until light and fluffy. Add the ground espresso and mix, then mix in the chocolate mixture. Mix in the dry ingredients and the remaining ¾ cup chocolate chips. Let the dough firm up in the refrigerator for 15–30 minutes.

3. Scoop the dough by heaping tablespoons onto a sheet pan and freeze. If you don't have room in your freezer for a sheet pan, simply scoop the cookies into a smaller pan or into a resealable plastic bag, then freeze, making sure the cookies do not clump together.✳

4. When ready to serve, heat the oven to 375 degrees. Butter a sheet pan very well or line it with parchment paper or a baking mat (or use a nonstick sheet pan). Without thawing the cookies, arrange them on the pan 2 inches apart and bake for 7 minutes. Serve warm.

✳ *The frozen cookie dough can be kept for up to 3 weeks. The cookies can be baked straight from the freezer.*

crunchy chocolate-almond toffee

SEE PHOTOGRAPH PAGE 59

I have recently discovered (and become totally addicted to) the marvelous Marcona almond, the favorite almond of Spanish chefs and tapas-lovers. I nibble them with wine before dinner; I add them to salads; I serve them with cheese; and I stick them into every dessert I can—sometimes all in one day! Marconas are tender and toasty, never hard and dry like some supermarket almonds. You can buy them online at *www.tienda.com*.

This combination of almonds with crunchy toffee and bittersweet chocolate is fantastic. You'll be amazed that you made it so easily—and so will any friends that you give it to! It makes a great holiday gift.

MAKES ABOUT 1 POUND

2 cups sugar

3 tablespoons light corn syrup

1$\frac{1}{2}$ cups (3 sticks) salted butter, cut into chunks

$\frac{1}{4}$ cup best-quality cocoa powder, such as Droste or Valrhona, sifted

1 cup whole blanched almonds, preferably Marcona (see above), toasted (see page 17) and roughly chopped

1. Line a sheet pan with sides with a nonstick baking mat, or oil it well with vegetable oil (or use a heavyweight nonstick sheet pan).

2. Pour the sugar into the center of a saucepan fitted with a candy thermometer. Pour $\frac{1}{4}$ cup water around the sugar and swirl gently to moisten it. Add the corn syrup and bring to a boil. Add the butter and boil until the mixture reaches 300 degrees. Turn off the heat and whisk in the cocoa, then stir in the nuts. Quickly pour the mixture onto the center of the prepared pan and let it spread out; it may not reach the sides. Set aside to cool at room temperature until completely hardened.

3. Using your hands (I wear gloves to avoid making fingerprints), pry the toffee out of the pan and break into large pieces. Store in an airtight container.*

* The toffee will keep well for up to 2 weeks.

{white chocolate– pecan blondies

This is one of the delicious little treats off the petit-four cart at Tru. It came to us along with my pastry assistant, Mike. Each chunky bite holds vanilla fudge studded with pecans and chocolate chips. To make perfect little squares, we trim off the edges before cutting, so I find that there are always bits of this irresistible buttery concoction in the kitchen to tempt me.

I purposely made this recipe quite large, because it's a perfect treat to make over the holidays. You can give some away, or take them to any party as a perfect dessert nibble.

MAKES 54 SMALL BARS

1 cup (2 sticks) unsalted butter
1 pound white chocolate, half of
   it broken into large chunks,
   the other half chopped
   (see page 15)
4 large eggs
1 cup sugar

1 teaspoon pure vanilla extract
1 large pinch of salt
2 cups all-purpose flour
$\frac{1}{3}$ cup chopped pecans
8 ounces ($\frac{2}{3}$ of a 12-ounce bag)
   semisweet chocolate chips

1. Line the bottom of a 16 × 10-inch sheet pan (with sides) with parchment or wax paper (or use 2 smaller pans). Heat the oven to 350 degrees.

2. Bring about an inch of water to a simmer in a saucepan. Combine the butter with the large chunks of white chocolate in a large bowl and set over the hot water, whisking to melt. In a separate bowl, whisk together the eggs, sugar, vanilla, and salt. Remove the bowl with the chocolate mixture from the heat, then whisk in the egg mixture. Mix in the flour, then the chopped white chocolate, pecans, and semisweet chocolate chips. Pour into the prepared pan. Smooth the top and bake for about 20 minutes, until set and very light golden brown. Let cool in the pan, then cut into 1½-inch × 2-inch bars. Store in an airtight container.*

These will keep for up to 3 days (you can cut into squares in advance, or just before serving).

oatmeal chocolate chip crisps

If you memorize one cookie recipe in your lifetime, this is the one to choose. It satisfies both chocolate-chip cookie lovers and oatmeal-raisin cookie lovers. I like to tinker with the classic recipes and try out all the flavors of chips and bits they keep inventing. There's a whole new world in the baking aisle since I was a kid: toffee chips, peanut butter chips, cinnamon chips, and more.

MAKES 4 TO 5 DOZEN

3 cups rolled oats (not quick-cooking)
1 cup (2 sticks) unsalted butter, slightly softened
1 1/2 cups light brown sugar, packed
2 large eggs

2 teaspoons pure vanilla extract
1/2 teaspoon baking soda
1/4 teaspoon salt
1 bag (about 10 ounces) miniature chocolate or cinnamon chips

1. Heat the oven to 300 degrees. Line a sheet pan with parchment paper or a non-stick baking mat (or use a heavyweight nonstick pan).

2. Put 2 cups of the oatmeal in the food processor and process it until finely ground and floury.

3. In a mixer fitted with the paddle attachment, cream the butter until soft and smooth. Mix in the brown sugar. Add the eggs and vanilla and mix until well blended. In another bowl, stir together both the ground and the whole oatmeal, the baking soda, and the salt. With the mixer running at low speed, add the dry ingredients to the batter and mix just until blended. Add the chocolate chips and mix just until blended. *

4. Drop by teaspoonfuls onto the pan, leaving 2 to 3 inches between them, as they will spread. Bake for 13 to 15 minutes, until lightly browned. Let cool on the pan, then store in an airtight container.

The cookie dough can be made and kept refrigerated for up to 3 days before baking. Or you can make lumps of dough and freeze them in a locked plastic bag, then take them out for baking a few at a time. Add an extra minute to the baking time.

cinnamon twists
with chocolate-peanut sauce

These cinnamon-spiked twists of puff pastry are incredibly easy to make and versatile to serve. They have the same light crispiness as my favorite cheese sticks, in a flaky, sweet-and-spicy cookie. They are delicious plain, or more luxurious and fun when dipped into a sweet sauce or stuck into a scoop of your favorite ice cream. You can also skip the sauce and add finely chopped nuts of your choice to the cinnamon-sugar mixture.

Frozen puff pastry is the best quick trick for speeding up all kinds of pastry and tart recipes. It's available at most supermarkets.

MAKES ABOUT 24 TWISTS

For the twists
$1/3$ **cup sugar**
1 teaspoon cinnamon
1 sheet of frozen puff pastry,
   thawed in the refrigerator
8 tablespoons (1 stick) unsalted
   butter, melted

For the sauce
1 cup milk
$1/4$ **cup sugar**
2 ounces semisweet or milk
   chocolate, coarsely chopped
   (see page 15)
$3/4$ **cup smooth peanut butter**

1. Make the twists: Line a sheet pan with parchment paper or a nonstick baking mat, or use a heavyweight nonstick pan. In a small bowl, toss the sugar and cinnamon together. Unroll or unfold the pastry onto a lightly floured surface and roll a rolling pin over the surface to make it lie flat and smooth out any creases.

2. Brush the pastry with all the melted butter and sprinkle the cinnamon sugar evenly over the surface. Working crosswise (cutting lines parallel to the shorter side of the pastry), use the tip of a sharp knife or a pizza cutter to cut the pastry into $1/2$-inch strips.

3. Lift up one end of each strip and twist it a few times, making long corkscrews (make about 4 turns per strip). Transfer to the prepared pan and press both ends down onto the pan to secure the twists (this will prevent them from untwisting as they bake). Refrigerate the twists for 15 minutes. *

4. Heat the oven to 400 degrees. Bake the twists for about 20 minutes, or until puffed and golden brown.

5. Make the sauce: Heat the milk and sugar to a simmer. Place the chocolate in a bowl and pour the hot milk over it, whisking until smooth and melted. Whisk in the peanut butter until smooth. Keep warm in the saucepan, or refrigerate✳✳ and reheat in the microwave for 1 to 2 minutes when ready to serve.

6. To serve, arrange the twists on a tray and pour the sauce into one big bowl or individual dipping bowls.

✳ *The unbaked twists can be refrigerated for up to 12 hours or frozen for up to a week.*

✳✳ *The sauce can be refrigerated for up to a week.*

lavender shortbread

I had to master the art of shortbread-making when I worked at Stapleford Park, an elegant hotel in the English countryside: Shortbread was served every single day, both at teatime and at bedtime. I enjoyed experimenting with subtle changes to the buttery flavor, and this is one of my favorites. The piney lavender gets smoothed out by the rich butter and sugar. You can easily buy fresh or dried lavender at spice markets and natural-food stores; just make sure whatever you use is intended for cooking.

My quick trick for shortbread is that you can skip rolling out the dough and just press it into a nonstick pan with your fingers. It won't look quite as perfect, but it will still taste great.

8 tablespoons (1 stick) cold
  unsalted butter, cut into pieces
¼ cup plus 2 tablespoons sugar
1 cup all-purpose flour

¼ cup cornstarch
¼ teaspoon salt
1 tablespoon dried or fresh
  lavender flowers (see headnote)

1. Heat the oven to 350 degrees. Line an 8- or 9-inch square baking pan with parchment paper (butter the pan lightly first to keep the paper from crumpling).

2. Cream the butter until soft (see page 16) in a mixer fitted with a paddle attachment. Add the ¼ cup sugar and mix until incorporated. Stir together the flour, cornstarch, and salt in a medium bowl. Add the dry ingredients to the butter mixture and mix at low speed just until the ingredients are almost incorporated, then add the lavender and mix until the dough starts to come together. Remove the bowl from the mixer and knead the dough a few times in the bowl with your hands, to bring the dough together and smooth it out.

3. Use your hands to press the dough evenly into the pan. Prick the shortbread all over with a fork to prevent buckling or shrinking.* Sprinkle the surface evenly with 1 tablespoon of the remaining sugar.

4. Bake for 15 minutes. After 15 minutes, deflate the dough by knocking the pan once against the oven rack, then rotate the pan to ensure even cooking and a flat surface. Bake for 10 to 15 minutes more, until light golden all over (it will not brown). As soon as the shortbread comes out of the oven, sprinkle the surface evenly with the remaining tablespoon of sugar. Let the shortbread cool for about 5 minutes.

5. Using a very sharp knife, cut the shortbread into bars or wedges, about 1½ inches by 3 inches. Let cool completely in the pan, then remove carefully and store in an airtight container.**

 * *The pressed-out dough can be covered and refrigerated for up to 2 days. Bring it to room temperature before baking.*
** *The finished cookies will keep for up to a week.*

langues-de-chat

For almost any occasion, you can't go wrong with ice cream and cookies for dessert. And with so many delicious, high-quality ice creams on the market (look for brands like Ciao Bella, Godiva, and Starbucks for unusual flavor choices), serving them to guests is a great idea. Dressing it up with a little homemade cookie makes the dessert complete. Or, forget about the ice cream and just serve the cookies smeared with Nutella or jam, or with hot fudge sauce (see page 30) for dipping.

Molds for langues-de-chat (cat's tongues) are wide at both ends and narrow in the middle, almost like a cartoon dog's bone; you might see them at fancy cookware stores or tag sales. But you can just pipe the cookies onto lined sheet pans. The cookies are pictured on page 112.

MAKES 80

6 tablespoons (³/₄ stick) cool unsalted butter, cut into pieces
1¼ cups confectioners' sugar, sifted
Scant ½ cup egg whites (from about 3 large eggs)
1 teaspoon pure vanilla extract
1 teaspoon pure lemon extract
³/₄ cup all-purpose flour

1. Heat the oven to 350 degrees.

2. Cream the butter until very smooth in a mixer fitted with a paddle attachment. (See page 16 for tips.) Mix in the sugar. A little at a time, mix in the egg whites, then add the extracts. Add the flour and mix just until incorporated.*

3. Transfer the batter to a pastry bag fitted with a ¼-inch plain tip. Pipe dough into buttered langue-de-chat molds (see above) or pipe in 2½-inch lengths onto sheet pans lined with nonstick baking mats. (If you don't have baking mats, use parchment paper.) Bake until golden on top and golden brown around the edges, about 10 minutes. Let cool on the pan (the cookies will crisp up as they cool) and store in an airtight container.**

* *The cookie batter can be refrigerated for 2 days before baking. Let it come to room temperature before piping.*

** *The baked cookies will stay crisp for 3 to 5 days in an airtight container.*

panna cotta rice pudding

I think I've tried every possible way to make rice pudding. You can make it on the stove, in the oven, with or without eggs, with raw or cooked rice. This is the method I developed to make a light, not starchy rice pudding in which you can actually taste and feel the rice. The idea of using gelatin and cream is borrowed from *panna cotta*, a light Italian version of custard.

Use any kind of dried fruit you have, and any kind of long-grain rice, such as Carolina, jasmine, or basmati. Short-grain rices, such as Arborio, are too starchy for this pudding.

MAKES 6 TO 8 SERVINGS

$^3/_4$ **cup basmati or other long-grain rice**
1 orange
2 cups milk
1 cup sugar
$^1/_4$ **teaspoon pure vanilla extract**

1 tablespoon unflavored dry gelatin
2 cups heavy cream, whipped
$^1/_2$ **cup chopped dried plums, apricots, or raisins, plumped in boiling water and drained**

1. In a heavy saucepan, combine the rice with 1½ cups water and bring to a boil over high heat. Stir, cover tightly (with a lid or foil), and turn down the heat as low as it will go. Cook for 20 minutes, then turn the heat off and let the rice sit for 5 to 10 minutes to allow it to absorb all the moisture evenly.

2. Meanwhile, using a sharp knife or vegetable peeler, peel the zest off the orange in wide strips, avoiding the white pith as much as possible. In a saucepan, heat the orange zest, milk, and sugar to a simmer and simmer until the sugar is dissolved. Sprinkle the gelatin over 1 tablespoon cold water and allow to soften. Turn off the heat. Add the gelatin to the hot liquid and whisk to dissolve the gelatin. Whisk the vanilla extract in.

3. Fill a large bowl with ice and cover the ice with cold water. Pour the hot mixture into a medium-size metal or glass bowl. Rest the base of the bowl in the ice water. Chill, stirring often, until the mixture starts to thicken. Remove the vanilla bean and orange zest. Fold in the whipped cream. Then fold in the rice and dried fruit.

4. While the mixture is still soft, divide among serving cups or transfer to a serving bowl. Refrigerate until chilled and firm.✳

✳ *Can be refrigerated for up to 3 days.*

peach and polenta
upside-down cake

I often sneak a little polenta into my cake batters: I love the sunny yellow color and nutty flavor it adds. It's worth looking for coarse-ground or stone-ground cornmeal; the flavor is much better and "cornier" than supermarket cornmeal. The flavor of sweet corn is delicious with summer fruits like peaches, apricots, plums, and especially white peaches if you can find them.

Upside-down cake is such an easy way of making a simple, wholesome cake that shows off the delights of seasonal fruit. You can prep it a day in advance, then bake it just before dinner to serve it all warm and saucy. The topping becomes a delicious and satisfying rich butterscotch sauce, mixed with the juices of the succulent fruit.

MAKES 8 TO 10 SERVINGS

For the topping
6 tablespoons (3/4 stick) salted butter
1/2 cup light brown sugar
2 peaches, each cut into 6 to 8 thick
    wedges

For the batter
8 tablespoons (1 stick) salted butter,
    softened

2/3 cup light brown sugar
2 large eggs
1 cup sour cream
2 teaspoons pure vanilla extract
    (optional)
1/3 cup uncooked polenta or
    coarse-ground cornmeal
1 1/3 cups all-purpose flour
2 teaspoons baking powder

1. Make the peach topping: Over low heat, melt the butter in a flame-proof 9- or 10-inch round cake pan, then turn off the heat and whisk in the sugar until blended. (The mixture may look curdled; this is okay.) Arrange the peach slices on top, in concentric circles. Set aside.

2. Make the batter: Cream the butter (see page 16) in a mixer fitted with a whisk attachment until light and fluffy. Add the sugar and mix well. Mix in the eggs one at a time, scraping down the bowl between additions. Add the sour cream and vanilla, if using, and mix; the batter may look a little curdled. At low speed, mix in the dry ingredients. Gently pour the batter over the peach slices and carefully spread the batter to cover.*

3. Heat the oven to 375 degrees. Place the cake pan on a sheet pan. Bake in the center of the oven until firm to the touch and golden, about 45 minutes. Remove and let cool for 10 to 15 minutes. Place a serving platter over the pan, hold them tightly together, and quickly flip them over to invert the cake onto the platter. Serve warm if possible.

✱ *The cake can be assembled up to this point and refrigerated overnight. If baking from the refrigerator, increase the baking time to 60 minutes. Once baked, the cake will keep at room temperature for 2 days.*

chai-spiced cheesecake

Chai is the Hindi word for tea. It is made in India by simmering tea, milk, sugar, and spices into an irresistibly aromatic brew that has quickly become very popular in this country.

The list of wonderful spices in *chai* may include allspice, black pepper, cardamom, cinnamon, cloves, coriander seed, ginger, mace, nutmeg, star anise, fennel seed, bay leaf, and vanilla bean. But you can also make a simple mix of just cardamom and Chinese five-spice powder, which is available at any Asian market. You can buy a good chai spice mixture at *www.worldspice.com,* and chai extract is also available; just stir it into the batter to taste.

MAKES 10 TO 12 SERVINGS

1½ cups walnuts, toasted (page 17) and cooled
¼ cup granulated sugar
3 tablespoons unsalted butter, melted
2 pounds cream cheese, at room temperature
1¼ cups brown sugar (dark or light)

4 large eggs
½ cup heavy cream
1 to 2 tablespoons finely ground chai spices (see above), or a mixture of Chinese five-spice powder and ground cardamom

1. Pulse the nuts and granulated sugar together in the food processor until crumbly. Stir in the melted butter and refrigerate.*

2. Heat the oven to 375 degrees. Butter a 9- or 10-inch springform pan. Use your fingers to press the walnut crust mixture into the bottom of the pan. Bake for 7 minutes. Let cool for at least 15 minutes (or completely) before adding the filling.

3. Reduce the oven temperature to 300 degrees. In a mixer fitted with a whisk attachment, whip the cream cheese until fluffy. In order, mix in the remaining ingredients, adding 1 tablespoon of the spice mixture to start. Taste and add more spice until the mixture is flavored to your liking.

4. Pour into the prepared pan. Bake until slightly puffed and barely shimmying in the center, about 50 minutes. Let cool at room temperature and then refrigerate in the pan, covered, until ready to serve.** To serve, remove the sides of the pan.

 * *The crust mixture can be made up to 1 week in advance.*
 ** *The finished cake can be covered and refrigerated for up to 3 days.*

elsie's quick apple coffee cake

This is the recipe everyone needs after the apple-picking outings of autumn—an easy, chunky, tasty apple cake that you can make often and never get tired of. My son, Gio, loves using the long pole with the net on the end to reach apples, so we always end up with extra bushels.

This recipe comes from my grandma Elsie's recipe file. It's good for breakfast, with afternoon tea, or as a homey dessert after a hearty soup-and-salad dinner. If you like plenty of sugary streusel crust on top (I do!), make this topping recipe, but Elsie's recipe called for half as much.

MAKES 1 CAKE

For the cake
1½ cups sifted all-purpose flour
2¼ teaspoons baking powder
½ cup sugar
½ teaspoon ground cinnamon
1 large egg, beaten
½ cup milk
4 tablespoons salted butter, melted
2 cups peeled, chopped apples
    (from about 3 apples)

For the topping
½ cup sugar
¼ cup flour
2 tablespoons cold salted butter,
    cut into small pieces
1 teaspoon ground cinnamon

1. Heat the oven to 400 degrees. Butter an 8-inch square baking dish.

2. Make the cake: In a large bowl, sift the sifted flour with the baking powder, sugar, and cinnamon. In another bowl, mix the egg, milk, and melted butter. Pour the wet ingredients into the dry ingredients, add the apples, and mix well. Pour into the prepared pan.

3. Make the topping: Pinch and mix the ingredients together with your fingers until crumbly. Sprinkle all over the top of the batter. Bake until golden and dry on top, 25 to 30 minutes. Let the cake cool in the pan and serve warm, cut into squares.*

* *The cake will keep for 3 to 4 days at room temperature.*

saffron
butter cake with orange glaze

I can never decide whether it's the color or the flavor of this cake that is more irresistible. The saffron and butter give it a rich yellow color and the orange glaze that soaks in is like pure sunshine. The glaze really makes the cake special (and also helps preserve it for up to a week), so do take that easy extra step. When I can get them, I use tart Seville oranges or exotic blood oranges in the glaze.

MAKES 1 CAKE

²/₃ cup orange juice
2 pinches of saffron
1¹/₂ cups all-purpose flour
1 teaspoon baking powder
¹/₂ teaspoon salt

1 cup (2 sticks) butter, slightly
   softened
1 cup plus ¹/₃ cup sugar
4 large eggs

1. Heat the oven to 350 degrees. Butter a large loaf pan or a 9-inch round cake pan and line the bottom with parchment paper.

2. In a small saucepan, bring the orange juice and saffron to a boil, then turn off the heat and set aside to steep.

3. In a medium bowl, combine the flour, baking powder, and salt. In a mixer fitted with a whisk attachment, or using a hand mixer, cream the butter until smooth (see page 16). Add 1 cup of the sugar and mix. With the mixer running at low speed, add the eggs one by one. Add half of the dry ingredients and mix. Add ¼ cup of the saffron-spiked orange juice and mix. Add the remaining dry ingredients and mix. Fish out any remaining saffron threads in the orange juice and mix them into the batter. (Reserve the remaining saffron-spiked orange juice.)

4. Pour the batter into the prepared pan and bake until the cake is raised and springy in the center and a tester inserted into the center comes out clean (a few crumbs are okay), 65 to 75 minutes for a loaf cake, 45 to 55 minutes for a round cake.

5. Meanwhile, make the glaze: Stir the remaining ¹/₃ cup sugar into the remaining saffron-spiked orange juice until the sugar is dissolved.

6. When the cake is done, let it cool in the pan for 15 minutes (it will still be warm). Run a knife around the sides of the pan. Set a wire rack on a sheet pan with sides (to catch the glaze) and turn the cake out onto the rack. Peel off the paper. Using a turkey baster or pastry brush, spread glaze all over the top and sides of the cake and let it soak in. Repeat until all the glaze is used. Let the cake cool at room temperature, then serve, or wrap in plastic and refrigerate.* Serve chilled or at room temperature, in thin slices.

Kept tightly wrapped and refrigerated, the cake will last up to a week. It can be frozen very successfully for up to 4 weeks, then thawed at room temperature.

banana maple tarte tatin

I learned from the famous French chocolatier and pastry chef Maurice Bernachon that people love to see black specks of vanilla bean in their desserts; it's proof that real vanilla beans were used in the recipe, and that always means better flavor. His tarte Tatin is traditional, with the exception of the whole vanilla bean baked right into the caramelized apple topping.

In this easy version of the French classic, I use maple syrup instead of making a caramel, and bananas (which don't really need cooking) instead of apples. The effect is still one of soft fruit, rich buttery juices, and crisp pastry. It makes an excellent fall or winter dessert, and happens to contain no added sugar. You can make it in a cake pan or even in a heavy frying pan.

MAKES 8 SERVINGS

1 sheet of frozen puff pastry, thawed overnight in the refrigerator

2 tablespoons unsalted butter

1/2 cup pure maple syrup

1/2 vanilla bean (use a whole vanilla bean, cut in half lengthwise)

2 to 3 bananas, sliced into 1/2-inch-thick coins

Vanilla ice cream, for serving

1. Choose a baking pan: Use a heavyweight 9- or 10-inch cake pan or a heavy oven-proof 10-inch skillet.

2. Unfold the pastry on a lightly floured work surface. Lightly roll a rolling pin over it to smooth out any creases and make it a little bit thinner. Using your pan as a guide, cut a round of dough that is about 1 inch bigger than the pan all the way around. Transfer the circle to a sheet pan, prick it all over with a fork, and keep it refrigerated.*

3. Heat the oven to 425 degrees. Meanwhile, put your pan on the stove and add the butter to it. Turn the heat to medium and heat until the butter is melted. Add the maple syrup and vanilla bean and bring to a boil, stirring occasionally. Turn off the heat and position the vanilla bean in the center of the pan. Arrange the banana slices (I like to place them in a spiral or in concentric circles) to cover the whole bottom of the pan.

4. Lay the pastry circle over the bananas, pressing the extra pastry around the sides of the pan so that it comes up the wall of the pan (rather than down around the bananas). The pastry will shrink during baking to fit the pan. Bake for 20 to 25 minutes, until the pastry is golden brown. Let cool in the pan for at least 30 minutes.**

5. Just before serving, warm the bottom of the pan for 1 or 2 minutes on the stove, over low heat (this will melt the caramel slightly and loosen the tart from the pan). Place a serving plate over the pan and quickly flip them over to turn the tart out, with the bananas facing up. Serve with vanilla ice cream, if desired.

The pastry circle can be refrigerated overnight or frozen for up to 2 weeks.

**Once baked, the tart should be served the same day it is made.*

blueberry turnovers

I am always on the lookout for a good turnover, one of my favorite treats—it's like a piece of pie that you can eat out of hand, with the same flaky-crust and juicy-fruit combo. I created these turnovers last summer, after picking pounds and pounds of blueberries from 6-foot-high bushes in Indiana with family and friends.

My quick trick for turnovers: A combination of fresh fruit and preserves makes a filling with the perfect texture—and you don't have to cook it! You can experiment with different flavor combinations, such as fresh peach chunks with raspberry preserves, fresh plums with cherry preserves, and so on. You can easily substitute blackberries or raspberries in this recipe.

MAKES 8

2 sheets of frozen puff pastry, thawed overnight in the refrigerator
¾ cup blueberry preserves
½ teaspoon pure vanilla extract
1 tablespoon cornstarch

4 tablespoons sugar, divided
½ teaspoon freshly grated lemon zest
1½ cups fresh blueberries
1 egg, beaten with 2 teaspoons water

1. Unfold the pastry on a lightly floured work surface. Using a rolling pin and pressing gently, roll out each pastry sheet into a 12 × 12-inch square; the pastry will become slightly thinner. Transfer to a cookie sheet, cover with plastic wrap, and refrigerate.

2. Heat the oven to 375 degrees. In a small bowl, stir together the preserves, vanilla, cornstarch, 2 tablespoons of the sugar, and the lemon zest. Fold in the fresh blueberries and keep refrigerated.

3. Using a sharp knife, cut each sheet of pastry into four 6-inch squares. Lay a pastry square on a work surface and brush the edges with the beaten egg wash. In the center of the square, place 2 heaping tablespoons of blueberry filling. Fold in half to create a triangle. Carefully press the edges together with your fingers, then crimp the edges with the tines of a fork to seal them well. Transfer to a sheet pan, placing them 1 inch apart, and keep refrigerated while you make the remaining turnovers.

4. Repeat with the remaining ingredients.*

5. Just before baking, brush the tops with egg wash and sprinkle with the remaining 2 tablespoons of sugar. Bake until golden brown, 20 to 25 minutes. Serve warm or let cool to room temperature. Serve the same day.

* *The unbaked turnovers can be refrigerated for up to 1 day or frozen (on a sheet pan or in resealable plastic bags) for up to a week. Transfer frozen turnovers to the refrigerator to thaw slightly about 4 hours before baking. When baking refrigerated or defrosted turnovers, you may need to increase the baking time by 5 to 10 minutes.*

lemon crostata
with fresh figs and goat cheese

Any time a dish—sweet *or* savory—doesn't taste quite perfect yet, or seems to need a little spark of something, I reach for a lemon. Lemon juice and zest breathe new life into flavors, bring zippy contrast to the sweetness of fruit, and add a note of springlike freshness to almost any recipe. Here, I use freshly grated zest to pick up the flavor of a basic tart crust— and it also perfumes the figs, mild goat cheese, and honey that are dotted on top.

Crostata is my favorite quick trick for making fruit tarts, because you can skip the tart pan altogether. On top of the crust, you can place almost any soft fruit or berry, as long as it isn't too juicy (orange sections or grapes, for example, would be too juicy).

MAKES 4 SERVINGS

1 cup all-purpose flour
¼ cup sugar
Freshly grated zest of ½ lemon
8 tablespoons (1 stick) cold
   unsalted butter, cut into pieces
1 egg, beaten

4 ounces mild, fresh goat cheese
10 ripe fresh figs (black or green),
   stems snipped off with a
   scissors, figs cut in half
   lengthwise
3 tablespoons honey

1. Make the dough: Blend the flour, sugar, and lemon zest at low speed in a mixer fitted with a paddle attachment. Add the butter and continue blending at low speed until the mixture is coarse and looks sandy. Add the egg and blend just until the mixture comes together. Form into a disc, wrap with plastic wrap, and refriger-ate for at least 1 hour. ✳

2. Heat the oven to 375 degrees. Butter a sheet pan very well, or line it with parch-ment paper or a baking mat (or use a heavyweight nonstick sheet pan).

3. On a floured surface, roll the dough out to a rough circle, 10 to 11 inches in diam-eter. The dough may seem crumbly, but push it back together as you roll and make patches if necessary. Transfer to the prepared pan. All around the dough circle, fold in the outer ½ inch of the circle to form a naturally raised "rustic" edge to the tart. Don't press the edge down.

4. Using your fingers, break the goat cheese into small pieces, sprinkling it over the bottom of the tart (not the folded edge). Arrange the fig halves in concentric circles over the goat cheese and drizzle the figs with 2 tablespoons of the honey. Bake for 25 to 30 minutes, or until the underside of the tart crust is browned. Brush the crust with the remaining honey as it comes out of the oven, and serve warm or at room temperature.

* *You can leave the dough in the refrigerator for up to 2 days; you can also remove it after 1 hour, roll it out, place it on the prepared pan, cover, and refrigerate for 2 days.*

pear and apple
streusel pie

You might think that a pastry chef would never let you get away with buying a pie crust—but I think it's much better to make a pie with a premade crust than not to make a pie at all! For the best flavor, always look for the ones made with at least some butter, rather than all shortening.

The most important thing about premade crusts is to place them in a glass pie dish for baking. Refrigerated crusts can be slipped right in; frozen ones should be defrosted and then transferred from the aluminum. This way, you can check the bottom crust as it bakes and make sure it's getting nice and golden—which to my mind is the most important step in pie-making. Nothing ruins a delicious pie—like this classic combination of autumn fruits and warm spices—faster than an undercooked, soggy bottom crust.

MAKES 1 PIE

For the streusel topping
¹⁄₂ cup all-purpose flour
¹⁄₄ cup light brown sugar, packed
¹⁄₄ teaspoon ground cinnamon
4 tablespoons (¹⁄₂ stick) cold unsalted butter, cut into pieces

For the pie
1 refrigerated or frozen 9-inch deep-dish pie crust (see above)

3 Granny Smith or other tart apples, peeled, cored, and sliced ¹⁄₄ inch thick
3 firm but ripe pears, peeled, cored, and sliced ¹⁄₄ inch thick
¹⁄₂ cup light brown sugar
1¹⁄₂ tablespoons cornstarch
¹⁄₄ teaspoon ground cinnamon
1 tablespoon cold butter, cut into small pieces

1. Make the topping: In a medium bowl, mix the flour, brown sugar, and cinnamon. Add the butter and, using your fingertips, pinch the ingredients together into a sandy, crumbly mixture. Do not overmix; as soon as the mixture is sandy, cover and refrigerate until ready to use.✲

2. If using a frozen crust, let it thaw at room temperature and gently remove the crust from the aluminum liner. Place in a glass pie dish. If using a refrigerated crust, use it to line a glass 9-inch deep-dish pie dish. Heat the oven to 375 degrees.

3. In a medium bowl, toss the apples, pears, brown sugar, cornstarch, cinnamon, and butter together. Place the filling in the pie crust. Sprinkle the streusel topping on top and place the pie on a sheet pan to catch any juices that might bubble over.

4. Bake for 40 to 50 minutes, until the crust is golden brown and the juices are bubbling. Check the pie after 30 minutes; if the streusel topping is already brown, cover lightly with foil. Let the pie cool for at least 30 minutes before serving. Serve warm or at room temperature.

✳ *You can mix the topping in advance and keep it refrigerated for up to 4 days.*

fruit potstickers

These make a wonderfully juicy dessert, especially after a stew or an Asian-inspired dinner. I always make fruit potstickers when I find myself with too many jam jars going at once. I am a sucker for jam and can never resist an unusual one (French plum jelly, special Sicilian marmalades, cherry preserves from Michigan; you name it, I have a jar of it in my refrigerator). When choosing your fruit, try to use whole berries or fruit that cooks quickly and isn't too juicy, like mango, banana, or pineapple. It's easy to adapt this recipe to smaller or larger groups: You can make eight dumplings or a hundred and eight, according to your needs.

All potstickers are dumplings, but all dumplings are not potstickers—only the ones that are cooked by this method of pan-frying, then steaming.

MAKES ABOUT 32

1 package (12 to 16 ounces) square wonton wrappers, available at many supermarkets and all Asian grocers

1/3 cup jam, preserves, or marmalade (see above)

1 pint whole strawberries (tops cut off), raspberries, banana slices, or canned mandarin orange sections, well drained (see above)

Vegetable oil, for frying

Sour cream, for serving

1. Lay out the wrappers on a work surface and place 1/2 teaspoon of jam in the middle of each one. Add one or two pieces of fruit (depending on how big your pieces are). Brush the edges with water and close as shown in the photo: Bring up all four corners and pinch them together in the center, then pinch all the seams closed.*

2. Heat 1/8 inch of oil in a heavy skillet with a tight-fitting lid (use two skillets if you need extra room) until very hot but not smoking. Place the potstickers in the oil and pan-fry until the bottoms are golden brown, about 2 minutes. Carefully add 1/4 cup water to the pan (the hot pan will spit) and place the lid on the pan. This will steam the dumplings and unstick them from the pan. Cook until the fruit is tender and the wonton skin is tender, 3 to 5 more minutes. Remove to a platter with a slotted spoon and serve immediately, with a dollop of sour cream on each plate for dipping.

The potstickers can be assembled up to 4 hours ahead and refrigerated, uncovered, on sheets of wax paper.

crisp
banana and pineapple fritters

I am an enthusiastic fan of panko, a flaky, white bread-crumb coating used for deep-frying in Japan. (Even though bread is not part of Japanese culinary tradition, Japanese cooks managed to invent the world's best bread crumbs!) Panko is available at some supermarkets and all Asian markets; the light, crisp crust it makes is truly a world apart from the usual bread-crumb coatings. This is a fast and easy dessert and would be great served with cheese or ice cream.

MAKES 4 TO 6 SERVINGS

2 large eggs
$1/8$ teaspoon ground cinnamon
2 cups panko (see above)
2 bananas, peeled and cut into 1-inch
   lengths

$1/2$ fresh pineapple, peeled with a
   sharp knife, cut into 1-inch pieces,
   and drained between paper towels
Vegetable oil, for frying
Honey, for drizzling

1. Whisk the eggs and cinnamon together in a shallow bowl. Spread the panko on a plate. One by one, dip the fruit pieces in the egg, roll in the panko, and set aside. Repeat the whole process one more time to build up a second coating.✻

2. Meanwhile, in a deep pot heat about 2 inches of oil to 365 degrees. Working in small batches to avoid crowding the pot, drop the fruit into the oil and cook, turning, until golden brown on all sides. Drain on paper towels or brown paper. Serve immediately, drizzled with honey.

✻ *The coated fruit can be refrigerated for up to 6 hours. But the fritters should be cooked at the last minute, straight from the refrigerator.*

phyllo birds' nests with mascarpone and raspberries

Strips of phyllo dough make beautiful golden nests to hold a variety of fillings. This is the easiest way I know to bake with phyllo: You don't even have to unroll it!

I garnish my nests with "micro mint," baby mint sprouts grown for us by Farmer Jones at the Culinary Vegetable Institute in Ohio. But other sweet herbs are just as good.

MAKES 8 SERVINGS

1 box (about 1 pound) frozen phyllo
  dough, thawed in the refrigerator
  overnight
4 tablespoons ($^1/_2$ stick) butter, melted
2 tablespoons sugar

6 to 8 ounces mascarpone, sour cream,
  or crème fraîche
$^1/_2$ pint raspberries
Confectioners' sugar and tiny or thinly
  sliced mint leaves, for garnish

1. Heat the oven to 350 degrees. Butter a sheet pan very well or line it with parchment paper or a nonstick baking mat (or use a nonstick sheet pan).

2. Remove the thawed phyllo from the box and remove the plastic wrapper. Place the roll on a cutting board. Using a large, sharp knife, cut across the roll into ¼-inch-wide strips, creating strips of dough about the same width as fettuccine pasta. Use slightly less than half of the roll, and set the rest aside for another project.

3. Run your fingers through the strips to remove all the wax paper that divides the phyllo sheets, separating and fluffing up the strips as you go. Divide the strips into eight reasonably equal piles. Lift each pile and mound it on the prepared pan. Each nest should be 3 to 4 inches across.

4. Spatter the nests lightly with melted butter, then sprinkle with sugar. Bake for 12 to 16 minutes, or until golden brown. Cool on the pan. Store in an airtight container.＊

5. Just before serving, place a teaspoon of mascarpone in the center of each dessert plate (this will hold the nest and keep it from sliding around on the plate). Place a nest on top, fill with mascarpone, and dot with raspberries. Sprinkle with confectioners' sugar, place a few mint leaves on top, and serve.

＊ *The nests will keep well in an airtight container at room temperature for up to 3 days.*

cool raspberry-lime terrine

In high summertime, a cool, tangy, quivery dessert is perfect. Fragrant lime and juicy raspberries combine in this pretty dessert, which also happens to be fat-free. You can make this in a loaf pan and serve it in slices, or, if you have any little dessert molds in your kitchen, this is a fun way to use them. I collect vintage molds that I always use for this recipe.

The frosted thyme sprigs look like little snow-covered branches. They are very easy to make and look very impressive, but of course they are completely optional.

MAKES 8 SERVINGS

For the terrine
1¼ cups sugar
3 tablespoons unflavored dry gelatin
1 cup freshly squeezed lime juice
2 to 2½ cups raspberries

For the garnish
1 egg white
2 tablespoons sugar
Fresh thyme sprigs

1. Make the terrine: Combine the sugar with 1¼ cups water in a saucepan. Bring to a simmer and stir to dissolve the sugar.

2. Meanwhile, spoon 2 tablespoons cold water into a small bowl and sprinkle the gelatin over the surface. Let soak, allowing the gelatin to absorb the water, about 3 minutes. Stir the gelatin mixture into the hot sugar syrup and stir to dissolve. Whisk in the lime juice and 2 cups more water.

3. Place the raspberries in a loaf pan or divide them among individual molds. Pour in the lime liquid. Refrigerate until chilled and firm, at least 3 hours.＊

4. Make the garnish: Whisk the egg white in a bowl. Spread the sugar out in a shallow bowl. Dip a thyme sprig in the egg white, shake off any excess, then dredge in the sugar. Set on a wire rack to dry for 30 minutes.＊＊

5. When ready to serve, dip the bottom of the pan into hot water for 10 seconds. Flip the terrine out onto a serving platter and garnish with thyme sprigs. Serve in slices.

＊ *The terrine can be refrigerated for up to 2 days.*
＊＊ *The sprigs can be made up to 1 day ahead and stored at room temperature, loosely covered.*

sugar roasted–lemon sorbet

A refreshing treat for lemon lovers. I sometimes find that fresh lemon sorbets are too tart; roasting the lemons in sugar and vanilla tames the tartness and makes the sorbet sweet, like a delicious little bite of candied lemon peel. It's easy to make little lemon-peel cups to serve the sorbet in, and the effect is very pretty.

My quick trick for juicing lemons is to microwave them first; the warmth releases the juice and softens the fibers, making it a snap to squeeze them.

MAKES 8 SERVINGS

18 lemons, scrubbed
2 cups sugar, plus more to taste

½ vanilla bean, halved lengthwise, insides scraped out with the tip of a sharp knife

1. Heat the oven to 375 degrees. Cut 14 of the lemons in half and place in a deep roasting pan. Sprinkle in the sugar and vanilla bean scrapings, and pour in water to just cover the lemons. Stir. Bake, stirring occasionally, for about 30 minutes, or until the edges of the lemons start to caramelize. Let cool to room temperature.

2. Cut the remaining 4 lemons in half and squeeze out the juice. Set the juice aside. If you like, make a serving cup out of each lemon half by using a sturdy teaspoon to scrape out the pulp and pith. Place the cups in the freezer.

3. Place a strainer over the bowl of a food processor (you can do this in the sink if you wish) and squeeze the roasted lemons into the strainer. Roughly chop 3 of the roasted lemon halves and add them to the food processor bowl; discard the rest. Purée until smooth.

4. Strain the mixture into another bowl and stir in 4 cups of water and ½ cup of the fresh lemon juice. Taste for sweetness and add sugar if needed: The mixture should taste just slightly too sweet at room temperature. When frozen, it will taste perfect. Refrigerate until cold (preferably overnight)* and freeze in your ice-cream maker. If using lemon cups, scoop the sorbet into the cups when it is still slightly soft and keep frozen until ready to serve.

* *The mixture can be kept refrigerated for up to 3 days. Once frozen, the sorbet is best the same day but will keep for up to a week.*

fudgy chocolate sorbet

Here is proof positive that you can satisfy a chocolate craving without butter and cream. Dark chocolate is intense without richness; it contains less dairy and cocoa butter than other chocolates, and more flavor-packed chocolate solids. I mix it with cocoa powder, the purest chocolate of all, for extra depth of flavor.

In this satisfying sorbet, the creaminess comes from the action of the ice-cream machine, not from rich ingredients.

MAKES 6 TO 8 SERVINGS

1 cup sugar
3⅓ cups warm water
3 ounces semisweet or bittersweet
    chocolate, melted (see page 14)
1 cup best-quality cocoa powder,
    such as Valrhona or Droste, sifted

2 teaspoons dark rum, Cognac,
    or brandy
Pinch of salt

Whisk the sugar and water together until completely dissolved. Place half of the sugar–water mixture in a bowl and whisk in the chocolate, cocoa powder, rum, and salt. Whisk in the remaining sugar–water mixture. Taste for sweetness and add sugar if needed: The mixture should taste just slightly too sweet at room temperature. When frozen, it will taste perfect. Refrigerate until cold (preferably overnight) and freeze in your ice-cream maker.*

* Once frozen, the sorbet tastes best the same day but will keep for up to a week.

lemon yogurt sherbet
with blackberry swirl

Sherbet is different from sorbet, not only in name, but in the recipe too. Sorbet is all fruit, while sherbet always contains a little bit of dairy—usually milk. This one has yogurt, which I often pair with lemon in my desserts. Somehow the tartness of both ingredients makes them get along well. Very sweet and intense summer berries, such as good ripe blackberries, are the natural balance for the sour elements. Together, they make for an aromatic, refreshing dessert, perfect after a backyard barbecue.

MAKES 8 SERVINGS

For the sherbet
1 cup sugar
2 cups freshly squeezed lemon juice
1 cup plain whole-milk yogurt

For the swirl
1 cup blackberries
3 tablespoons sugar

1. Make the sherbet mixture: Combine the sugar and 1 cup water in a saucepan and bring to a boil. Let cool slightly, then mix in the lemon juice and yogurt. Refrigerate until chilled.

2. Meanwhile, make the swirl: Combine the blackberries, 1 tablespoon water, and the sugar in a saucepan and bring to a boil. Reduce the heat to a simmer and cook, stirring often, until the mixture is reduced to a thick purée. Strain (if you wish; this will remove the seeds, but it is optional) and refrigerate until chilled (preferably overnight). *

3. Freeze the sherbet in an ice-cream maker and put a large bowl in the freezer to chill. When the sherbet is frozen but not hard, transfer it to the frozen bowl. Fold in the chilled blackberry purée, swirling it with a spatula. Keep frozen until ready to serve. **

 * The sherbet mixture and the swirl can be kept refrigerated for up to 3 days.

** Once frozen, the sherbet is best the same day but will keep for up to a week.

toasted almond sherbet with {sugar-frosted almonds

This is my humble tribute to the Good Humor Toasted Almond Bar. That treat is actually a tribute to the classic Italian dessert called *biscuit Tortoni,* although I didn't know that when I fell in love with it as a kid. When toasting the almonds for this recipe, go as dark as you dare. You want them to be mahogany in color to achieve the right flavor intensity.

The frosted almonds are optional. If not making them, you'll only need 2 cups of almonds.

MAKES 4 TO 6 SERVINGS

3 cups blanched or peeled whole almonds, such as Marcona (see page 67)

2 cups milk, plus a little extra as needed

2 cups simple syrup (see page 19)

1 vanilla bean, split lengthwise, insides scraped out with the tip of a sharp knife

$1/2$ cup sugar

Freshly grated zest of $1/4$ orange

Pinch of cinnamon

1. Toast the almonds on a sheet pan until golden and fragrant (see page 17). Remove 1 cup of the almonds and set aside to make the frosted almonds later. Return the remaining 2 cups almonds to the oven and toast until dark brown. Immediately, while still hot, combine them in a bowl with the milk, stir, and let cool to room temperature. Purée the mixture in a blender until very smooth and strain through a fine sieve. Measure the mixture and, if necessary, add more milk to make 2 cups. Whisk in the simple syrup and the scrapings from the vanilla bean. Refrigerate until cold (preferably overnight) and freeze in your ice-cream maker.

2. Make the frosted almonds: In a deep saucepan, combine the sugar, $1/4$ cup water, the orange zest, and cinnamon and bring to a boil. Add the reserved cup of almonds and simmer, stirring, as the water evaporates. The glaze will be shiny and transparent at first, then turn opaque as the water cooks away. When the nuts are completely coated with sugar crystals, they are done. Spread them out on a sheet pan to cool.* (To wash the saucepan, soak it overnight.)

3. Serve the sorbet with some almonds stuck into each dish.

* *Once frozen, the sorbet is best the same day but will keep for up to a week. The frosted almonds can be made 2 weeks in advance and stored in an airtight container.*

pistachio semifreddo

Pistachio is one of my favorite ice-cream flavors, but I can't find it in every ice-cream parlor the way I used to. So I make my own, with this voluptuously creamy Italian dessert (the word *semifreddo* means "semi-cold"). It is a lot quicker and easier to make than ice cream and just as good.

Traditionally, pastry chefs use a drop of almond extract as a quick trick to augment the subtle flavor of pistachios.

MAKES 6 TO 8 SERVINGS

5 ounces white chocolate, coarsely chopped (see page 15)

1½ cups heavy cream

½ cup shelled undyed pistachios, toasted (see page 17), cooled, and finely ground in a food processor

½ cup egg whites (from about 4 large eggs)

2 tablespoons sugar

½ teaspoon pure almond extract

1. Place the chocolate in a medium bowl. In a small saucepan, heat the cream and pistachios over medium heat just until boiling. Immediately turn off the heat. Pour the hot cream over the chocolate and whisk until melted and smooth. Cover and refrigerate for at least 6 hours.*

2. Remove the mixture from the refrigerator. Using a mixer fitted with a whisk attachment or a hand mixer, whip it into fluffy, soft peaks. Return to the refrigerator.

3. Set out 6 to 8 ramekins (see page 21). In a clean, dry bowl, whip the egg whites until soft peaks form, then add the sugar and continue whipping until glossy and stiff, about 30 seconds more. Fold into the white chocolate mixture with the almond extract, then spoon the mixture into the ramekins (or pipe through a pastry bag fitted with a large plain tip; see page 19). Smooth the tops. Freeze at least 4 hours or overnight.** For the best flavor and texture, let soften at room temperature for 10 minutes before serving.

* The cream and chocolate mixture can be refrigerated overnight.

** Once frozen, the semifreddos can be kept in the freezer for up to 4 days.

espresso granita and whipped cream shots

Dessert, coffee, and air-conditioning, scooped together in a glass. This cooling combination of frozen coffee and cream is sometimes served as breakfast in the hottest months of the Italian summer, sandwiched into a sweet roll. I find that a touch of vanilla and orange make the strong, dark coffee rounder in flavor.

MAKES 8 SERVINGS

½ **cup sugar**
½ **vanilla bean, split lengthwise**
2 **thick strips of orange zest, plus thin strips for garnish**
1 **cup brewed espresso or other very strong coffee**
1 **cup heavy cream, whipped**

1. Pour 1 cup water into a saucepan, add the sugar, vanilla bean, and orange zest, and bring to a boil. Turn off the heat and stir in the espresso. Strain into a shallow baking pan, cover, and freeze overnight, until solid.＊ At the same time, freeze a container to store the finished granita in. Using a sturdy metal spoon or fork (hold it by the side, not the handle), scrape down the length of the pan, shaving the mixture into icy flakes. As you work, transfer the granita to the frozen container. Store in the freezer until ready to serve.＊＊

2. To serve, fill small glasses with granita and top with a big dollop of whipped cream. Garnish with a small strip of orange zest.

＊ *The granita will keep for a week in the freezer, either before or after scraping.*

＊＊ *If you freeze it after the scraping, you may need to break it up a bit just before serving.*

Chocolate Tiramisù

Chocolate Malted Semifreddo

Peppermint Crunch
Ice Cream Sandwiches

Chocolate Pavlova

Towering Apple Tarts

Crisp Apple Hash Browns with
Ice Cream and Cider Sauce

Individual Pineapple Tarts

Plum Jam

Chips and Dip (Phyllo
Triangles with Lemon Curd)

Chilled Passionfruit Mousse

Cinnamon Crème Brûlée

Crème Caramel

Dried Plum and Almond
Phyllo Triangles

Crisp Phyllo Cigars with
Spiced Nut Filling

45-minute recipes

chocolate tiramisù

This Italian combination of fresh, mild *mascarpone* cheese, strong spiked coffee, delicate ladyfingers, and a sprinkling of chocolate is one of the world's truly great desserts. The flavors, of course, are delicious together, but there's also something about the light, fluffy, rich texture that causes people to lose their heads. Maybe that's why there's an entire website dedicated to lovers of tiramisù! My favorite recipe mixes even more chocolate right into the mascarpone.

For busy cooks, tiramisù is a great quick trick because it gives the same effect as a cake or custard dessert, with no cooking. You can buy mascarpone at gourmet stores or on the Internet.

MAKES 8 TO 10 SERVINGS

10 ounces best-quality semisweet chocolate, 8 ounces coarsely chopped (see page 15) and 2 ounces peeled into shavings with a vegetable peeler

2 cups heavy cream

8 ounces mascarpone

1/3 cup Kahlúa or other coffee liqueur

2 cups espresso or very strong brewed coffee, cooled

44 (approximately) ladyfingers (available at supermarkets and Italian bakeries)

Confectioners' sugar

1. The day before you plan to serve the tiramisù, place the chopped chocolate in a large bowl. In a saucepan, bring the cream to a simmer over medium-high heat. Pour the hot cream over the chocolate and let it sit for 1 minute, then whisk until the chocolate is melted. Whisk in the mascarpone, then strain the mixture into a bowl big enough to whip the mixture in the next day. Cover and refrigerate for at least 6 hours or overnight.*

2. Remove the chocolate mixture from the refrigerator and whip until fluffy and slightly stiffened, being careful not to overwhip (like heavy cream, the mixture can turn to butter if whipped too long). Keep refrigerated.

3. Combine the Kahlúa and espresso in a shallow dish and bring out a 9 × 13-inch dish to hold the tiramisù. I wear rubber gloves for the next step to keep my fingers from getting stained.

4. Pick up one ladyfinger, then place it in the espresso for just as long as it takes you to pick up the next one and place it in the espresso (about 10 seconds). Fish the first one out and place it in the bottom of the empty dish. Repeat until you have one complete layer of ladyfingers, arranging them in rows in the bottom of the dish and continuously adding and removing the ladyfingers from the espresso mixture. (This will allow them to soak for the perfect amount of time without getting soggy. They should be wet on the outside but still have an unsoaked core at the center.)

5. When you have covered the bottom of the dish, spread half of the chocolate mixture over the ladyfingers. Sprinkle the top evenly with half of the chocolate shavings. Repeat, making one more complete layer of ladyfingers, chocolate, and shavings. Cover and refrigerate the dessert until ready to serve, at least 2 hours.* Sprinkle the top with confectioners' sugar. Serve cold, in large spoonfuls.

* The dessert is at its best the next day, and will keep for 3 days.

chocolate malted
semifreddo

Elsewhere in this book, there's a kids' recipe for frozen chocolate pops that are a lot like Fudgsicles (see Frozen Milk Chocolate Pops, page 157). This is a more grown-up tribute to the same treat, with the same milky chocolate flavor and a deep, toasty undertone from the malt powder. Malt powder, made from barley, wheat, and milk, was invented in the 1870s by the Horlicks brothers, in Chicago. Like many new foods at the time, such as breakfast cereal and graham crackers, it was sold as a health food. But it's really just tasty.

Semifreddo is a frozen, creamy Italian concoction that you can easily make in a home freezer, with no ice-cream maker needed. The brandy adds flavor and also helps preserve the creamy texture: When a mixture contains alcohol, it will not develop icy crystals.

MAKES 8 TO 10 SERVINGS

4 large egg yolks
Scant $1/2$ cup sugar
2 tablespoons brandy
2 tablespoons vanilla-flavored malt
    powder (such as Carnation)
$1/3$ cup milk

$1/2$ vanilla bean, split lengthwise
3 ounces best-quality semisweet
    chocolate, chopped (see page 15)
$1^3/4$ cups heavy cream
Cocoa powder and confectioners'
    sugar, for garnish

1. Line 8 to 10 cups of a muffin tin with cupcake liners. Place in the freezer.

2. Whisk the egg yolks, sugar, brandy, malt powder, milk, and vanilla bean in the top of a double boiler or in a bowl. Place over simmering (not boiling) water and cook the mixture, whisking continuously, until very thick, 5 to 10 minutes.

3. Remove from the heat and discard the vanilla bean. Whisk in the chocolate to melt it and set aside to cool to room temperature. Once the mixture is cooled, whip the cream to soft peaks and fold into the chocolate mixture until completely combined. Divide the mixture among the lined cups. Freeze overnight.*

4. To serve, flip the semifreddos upside down onto dessert plates and peel off the liners. Let sit for 10 minutes before serving; the dessert will be more flavorful and creamy. Just before serving, use a sifter or small strainer to sprinkle the semifreddos lightly with cocoa powder and confectioners' sugar.

The semifreddos can be made and frozen up to 1 week in advance.

peppermint crunch ice cream sandwiches

I love all sandwiches—tea sandwiches, grilled sandwiches, burgers (such as the Cookie-burgers on page 148)—and I find myself inventing new dessert versions all the time. This recipe recreates the classic that started it all: the ice-cream sandwich of chocolate cookies and vanilla ice cream that I fell for as a child. I like to add a crunchy coating of peppermint candy to the outside (especially after Christmas, when I always seem to have lots of leftover candy canes). The sandwiches are very good without the peppermint candy, too.

This entire recipe is a perfect do-ahead project. You can speed up the process by using packaged dark-chocolate wafers instead of making your own. If you want the cookie crusts to be crisp, eat them the same day they are made. If you like yours softer, give them some time to mature in the freezer, at least overnight or up to two weeks.

MAKES 18 SANDWICHES

12 tablespoons (1½ sticks) salted butter, softened

¾ cup confectioners' sugar

2 teaspoons pure vanilla extract

¼ cup best-quality cocoa powder, such as Valrhona or Droste, sifted

2 tablespoons cornstarch

1 cup all-purpose flour

2 pints vanilla or another ice cream of your choice

1 cup crushed peppermint candy (made by putting candy canes or peppermint sticks in a resealable plastic bag, then whacking them with a rolling pin)

1. In a mixer fitted with the paddle attachment, cream the butter until soft and smooth (see page 16). Add the confectioners' sugar and continue mixing until well blended. Add the vanilla and mix until light and fluffy. In a separate bowl, stir together the cocoa powder, cornstarch, and flour. With the mixer running at low speed, add the dry ingredients to the butter mixture and blend just until combined. Form the dough into a disk, wrap it in plastic wrap, and chill for at least 2 hours. ✳

2. Heat the oven to 325 degrees. On a floured work surface, using a floured rolling pin, roll the dough out to ⅛ inch thick, or as thin as you can get it. (The dough will be a little crumbly and rough, but you can use your fingers to patch any holes.) Use flour-dipped cookie cutters to cut out circles 2 to 3 inches in diameter and place them on an ungreased sheet pan, leaving an inch between the cookies. Prick the cookies lightly with a fork. Bake until crisp, 12 to 14 minutes, then let cool on the pan. Reroll the dough scraps and keep making more cookies until you've used all the dough. Let all the cookies cool and store in an airtight container.*

3. To build the sandwiches, place a flat plate or small tray in the freezer. Scoop the ice cream into balls and place them on the frozen tray. Lay a large piece of plastic wrap over the ice cream balls and use a second tray (or the palm of your hand) to press them flat. Don't press them too thin; you want at least 1/2 inch of ice cream thickness. Return to the freezer again to firm up. Spread the peppermint candy out on a plate. Sandwich each ice cream disk between 2 cookies and roll the sides in the candy until coated. Wrap the sandwiches individually in foil, twist the ends, and freeze until ready to serve.**

* *The dough can be mixed and chilled for up to 3 days. Once baked, the cookies can be stored in an airtight container at room temperature for up to 1 week.*

** *The finished sandwiches can be kept in the freezer for up to 2 weeks.*

chocolate pavlova

A traditional Pavlova is a big white pillow of meringue, crisp on the outside, marshmallowy on the inside, and covered with whipped cream and fruit. When you add chocolate to the recipe, the meringue comes out with a brownie-like interior and a crackly crust. I like the combination of dark chocolate, cream, and strawberries, but you can use any fruit you like—or none at all. A bit of raspberry vinegar gives the meringue good depth of flavor and picks up the berries in the topping.

This baking method ensures a gradual cooling, which protects the delicate meringue from deflating too much.

MAKES 8 TO 10 SERVINGS

1/2 cup egg whites, at room temperature (from about 4 large eggs)

1/8 teaspoon salt

1 cup plus 2 tablespoons sugar

1 1/2 teaspoons cornstarch

1 tablespoon raspberry vinegar or red wine vinegar

1/4 cup best-quality cocoa powder, such as Valrhona or Droste (see page 15), sifted

1 cup heavy cream

1 cup sliced strawberries or whole raspberries, or any combination of ripe fruit

1. Heat the oven to 350 degrees.

2. In a mixer fitted with a whisk attachment, whip the egg whites and salt until foamy. Add the 1 cup sugar, cornstarch, and vinegar and continue whipping until stiff, smooth, and glossy, about 5 minutes more. Add the sifted cocoa powder and mix just to combine, 10 to 20 seconds more.

3. Cut a piece of parchment paper to fit into a sheet pan. Use a pencil to draw or trace a circle 9 inches in diameter on the paper. Line the sheet pan with the paper, pencil side down (you should still be able to see the circle). Spoon the egg whites into the circle and use the back of the spoon to smooth the top and sides of the disk.

4. Bake in the center of the oven for 10 minutes, then reduce the heat to 300 degrees and bake until the meringue has puffed up and cracked on the top, about 45 minutes more. Turn off the oven, prop the oven door open, and let the meringue cool in the oven for at least 30 minutes, to room temperature. *

5. When you're ready to serve, whip the cream with the remaining 2 tablespoons sugar. Place the meringue on a serving platter and pile the whipped cream on top, spreading it evenly to within $\frac{1}{2}$ inch of the edge of the meringue. Arrange the fruit on top of the cream. To serve, slice into wedges with a serrated knife.

* *The meringue can be held at room temperature for a few hours before serving.*

towering apple tarts

Apple tart is a dessert that I never get tired of making—or eating. Chunky ones, thin ones, fancy ones, rustic ones, I love them all. This is one of my old favorites, taught to me by three-star Michelin chef Nico Ladenis at his London restaurant. Nico is known for his strict devotion to the French classics. This is, therefore, the perfect individual apple tart. It is in the French *tarte fine* style, which always means very delicate, thin slices of fruit.

MAKES 8

1 sheet of frozen puff pastry, thawed in the refrigerator
8 Granny Smith or other tart, firm apples

$1/2$ cup sugar
$1/2$ teaspoon ground cinnamon
4 tablespoons ($1/2$ stick) cold unsalted butter

1. Unfold the pastry on a lightly floured work surface. Using a rolling pin, roll the pastry out, until very thin, less than $1/8$ inch thick. (If the pastry seems to be getting too soft, transfer it to a sheet pan and chill for 30 minutes, then return it to the work surface.) Use a biscuit cutter or an inverted glass to cut out eight $3^1/2$-inch disks. Line a sheet pan with parchment paper, or use a heavyweight nonstick sheet pan. Arrange the disks on the pan and chill.

2. Peel, core, and halve the apples. Slice the apple halves very, very thin (if you have a mandoline, use it). Toss the sugar and cinnamon together in a bowl. Cut the butter into 16 reasonably equal chunks.

3. To assemble the tarts, place a chunk of butter in the center of a pastry disk and sprinkle with cinnamon sugar. Stack the apple slices in an overlapping spiral pattern around the butter, starting with the larger slices and working your way up with smaller ones. Every inch or so, sprinkle the apples with cinnamon sugar. Each finished tart should be about 3 inches high and be shaped like a beehive or igloo (see photo). Place another chunk of butter on the top and sprinkle the tarts liberally one more time with cinnamon sugar. Keep refrigerated until ready to bake. ✱

4. Heat the oven to 375 degrees. Bake the tarts until golden brown and tender, about 30 minutes. Serve warm.

✱ *The recipe can be made up to this point and frozen for up to 2 weeks.*

crisp apple hash browns
with ice cream and cider sauce

One of the best presents I ever received was a little Japanese slicing device, much lighter and cheaper than a traditional mandoline, that instantly reduces fruits and vegetables to heaps of perfect matchsticks. I've successfully attacked apples, pears, cucumbers, potatoes, fennel, and more. You can easily find an inexpensive one at any Asian cooking market or website; those made by Benriner are of good quality and value.

To make this unusual but easy dessert, I just gather the apple matchsticks into rounds, then spatter them with butter and sugar and bake until browned and lightly chewy. They look a lot like hash-brown potatoes, but they taste sweet and crisp. Vanilla ice cream and a cider "sauce"—really just apple cider reduced until thick and jammy-tasting—round out the simple yet elegant plate.

MAKES 4

5 tablespoons unsalted butter (or ¼ cup melted clarified butter, available at gourmet stores or at Indian markets)
3 Granny Smith apples (do not peel)

¼ cup confectioners' sugar, plus extra for garnish
2 cups apple cider
1 pint caramel, vanilla, or cinnamon ice cream, slightly softened

1. If starting with regular butter, slowly melt it over low heat until the golden butter-fat separates from the cloudy white milk solids. The solids will sink to the bottom of the pan. Carefully pour off the golden liquid into a bowl and discard the solids. You have just made clarified butter!

2. Use a heavyweight nonstick sheet pan, or cover a sheet pan with a nonstick baking mat.

3. Halve and core the apples, then julienne into thin sticks, like potato sticks or matchsticks (see headnote). On the prepared pan, gather the apple sticks into 8 patties about 3 inches in diameter and not more than ½ inch thick. It's important to keep the patties the same thickness all the way across, not thicker or thinner in some spots.

4. Heat the oven to 250 degrees. Lightly drizzle the patties with clarified butter, then sprinkle well with the ¼ cup confectioners' sugar. Bake for about 90 minutes, or until golden around the edges. Let cool on the pans. Store the hash browns in an airtight container until ready to serve.✳

5. To make the sauce, simmer the cider in a small sauce pan until it becomes a thick golden syrup (this will take 45 minutes to an hour). Let cool until ready to serve.**

6. To serve, place one hash brown on a dessert plate, top it with a scoop of ice cream, and carefully place another one on top as a lid. Press down gently. Spoon a "swoosh" of cider reduction on the plate and sprinkle the whole thing with confectioners' sugar.

 * *The hash browns will stay crisp in an airtight container for up to 2 days.*

 ** *The sauce can be refrigerated for up to 1 week; serve it warm or at room temperature.*

individual
{pineapple tarts

From looking at the photo, you may not believe that you can make these—but you can, and quickly! This is a classic tart from the famous French pastry chef Gaston Lenôtre. I learned it when I was just starting out as a chef, and I ended up making them all the time: Individual tarts are perfect for any buffet or party. You don't have to do any slicing up or portioning out, and they can be filled with any fruit that doesn't need cooking, such as berries or kiwi fruit. Or you can leave out the fruit altogether and make an easy chocolate filling such as the one for Chocolate Tiramisù (page 110).

MAKES 9

4 ounces cream cheese, slightly
   softened at room temperature
2 tablespoons confectioners' sugar
1 teaspoon rum
1 sheet of frozen puff pastry, thawed
   in the refrigerator

$\frac{1}{4}$ of a fresh pineapple, sliced
   crosswise $\frac{1}{2}$ inch thick, or 1 can
   (about 14 ounces) pineapple
   rings, well drained
5 candied (glacéed) cherries, or
   maraschino cherries, halved
$\frac{1}{3}$ cup apricot jam (for the glaze;
   optional)

1. To make the filling, whip the cream cheese in a mixer until light and fluffy. Whip in the confectioners' sugar and rum. Refrigerate.

2. To make the tart shells, dust a work surface lightly with flour and roll over the puff pastry with a rolling pin, pressing lightly to make it a little thinner. You want to end up with a roughly 9 × 9-inch square. Refrigerate for about 20 minutes.

3. Line a sheet pan with parchment paper or nonstick baking mats, or use a nonstick sheet pan. Using the tip of a very sharp knife, cut the pastry into 3-inch squares. Fold each square in half diagonally, making a triangle, and cut a band around the edge, ¼ inch wide, as though you are trying to cut a ¼-inch frame around the pastry square—but do not detach the center. Leave the center square connected at the corners (see photograph).

recipe continues ➡

4. Unfold the square on the prepared pan. Paint the edges with water. Fold back the corners of the frame over each other, attaching each corner to the opposite side (see photo). Prick the bottom of the tarts and refrigerate for 20 minutes.*

5. Meanwhile, heat the oven to 425 degrees. Bake the tarts in the top third of the oven until golden brown, 12 to 15 minutes. Let cool on the pan. If the centers have puffed during the baking, press them down to deflate.

6. Once the tart shells have cooled, and when you are ready to serve, spoon the cream cheese mixture into the centers. Top with sections of pineapple and place half a cherry at opposite corners (see photo). You can serve the tarts as is, or make a shiny glaze for the top. To make the glaze, mix the apricot jam with 2 tablespoons water in a saucepan and bring to a simmer. Brush the mixture over the fruit to glaze the tarts. Let the glaze set for at least 3 minutes and serve as soon as possible.**

* *The unbaked tart shells can be covered and refrigerated for up to 2 days, or wrapped and frozen for up to 3 weeks.*

** *Once filled, the finished tarts should be served within 4 hours.*

plum jam

I learned to make jam from my cooking school friend Madelaine Bullwinkel, who makes the best jams of anyone I know. Once you understand how it works, it's easy to do it!

First you heat the fruit to encourage it to release its juice. You mix that juice with an equal amount of sugar (which is less sugar than most recipes call for). You cook the mixture down until there's enough pectin (natural fruit gelatin) to cause the juice to jell. Then you put the fruit back in the liquid and simmer until it reabsorbs the pectin-heavy juice.

MAKES ABOUT 6 CUPS

**3 pounds dark-purple Italian plums
(also called prune plums),
quartered and pitted (do not peel)**

**Sugar
1½ tablespoons freshly squeezed
lemon juice**

1. Combine the cut-up plums and 1 cup water in a heavy 5-quart saucepan (do not use aluminum or unfinished cast iron). Bring to a boil, then reduce the heat to a steady simmer, cover, and cook for 20 minutes.

2. Pour the mixture through a strainer set over a bowl to catch the juices, letting it drain for 15 minutes. Measure the drained juices. Measure out the same amount of sugar. Return the juices to the saucepan and bring them to a boil. Note the temperature of the boiling mixture; this is the "boiling point," and you'll need to remember it later. Add 1 tablespoon of the lemon juice and begin adding the sugar ½ cup at a time, allowing the mixture to return to a boil before adding the next ½ cup sugar. Continue cooking until the liquid reaches its jell point, which is 8 degrees hotter than the boiling point. This takes 5 or 10 minutes.

3. Turn off the heat and stir in the plum pieces. Let the fruit and liquid steep together for 15 minutes. Return the preserves to a boil. Stir in the remaining ½ tablespoon lemon juice and boil for about 10 minutes, stirring frequently and making sure you reach the bottom of the pan, until the temperature rises to 215 degrees. Turn off the heat and skim off any foam. Let cool, then transfer to jars or other airtight containers. Keep refrigerated.*

* The jam will last in the refrigerator for at least 2 weeks (or, to preserve it for longer, find instructions for canning in **The Joy of Cooking** *or any book on preserving foods).*

chips and dip
(phyllo triangles with lemon curd)

Crispy chips with a creamy dip—it's everyone's favorite snack. Here's my dessert version, with a smooth, tangy-sweet lemon curd and flaky triangles of phyllo dough. "Curd" is the British name for this mixture of eggs, sugar, butter, and lemon, because it has the creamy texture of fresh cheese curds; but it has nothing to do with cheese. Lemon curd keeps very well in the refrigerator and is delicious on toast or crumpets—it's like butter and jam in one. You can also serve the lemon curd with Langues-de-Chat (page 76) or thin store-bought cookies for dipping.

Most lemon curd recipes call for constant stirring, but my quick trick here is to use whole eggs instead of egg yolks; you can be sure that the mixture won't curdle or break.

MAKES 8 TO 12 SERVINGS

For the lemon curd
2 large eggs
$\frac{1}{2}$ cup sugar
Freshly grated zest of $\frac{1}{2}$ lemon
$\frac{1}{3}$ cup freshly squeezed lemon juice
2 tablespoons cold unsalted butter,
 cut into pieces

For the phyllo triangles
3 sheets frozen phyllo dough, thawed
 in the refrigerator (see page 18)
4 tablespoons ($\frac{1}{2}$ stick) unsalted
 butter, melted
6 tablespoons sugar

1. Make the lemon curd: Bring about an inch of water to a simmer in a medium to large saucepan. In a mixer fitted with a whisk attachment, whisk the eggs and sugar together until very light yellow and fluffy. Whisk in the lemon zest and lemon juice. Rest the mixing bowl in the saucepan, with the bowl's base resting *above* (not in) the simmering water. (This will cook the mixture very slowly.) Cook, whisking occasionally, until the mixture is thickened and custardy, 10 to 15 minutes. Remove the bowl from the pan and stir in the butter until melted. Transfer to a container, let cool, cover, and refrigerate for at least 2 hours.*

2. Make the phyllo triangles: Heat the oven to 350 degrees. Line a large sheet pan with parchment paper. Place 1 sheet of phyllo on the pan and brush with melted butter. Sprinkle evenly with 2 tablespoons of sugar, then place another sheet of phyllo on top. Brush with melted butter, sprinkle with sugar, lay another sheet of phyllo on top, brush with melted butter, and sprinkle with sugar.

3. With the tip of a sharp knife, cut the stack into 2-inch-wide rows, then cut the rows into triangles. Cover with parchment paper. Place another sheet pan on top. (This is to keep the phyllo from buckling during baking, so the top pan should not be too lightweight. Weigh it down slightly if necessary.)

4. Bake for 10 to 12 minutes, until the phyllo is golden brown. Let cool before unstacking the pans. Once cooled, remove the chips from the pan (each chip will consist of three baked-together layers of phyllo) and store them in an airtight container.**

5. Serve the chips on a platter with the bowl of lemon curd next to it, or make individual plates with ramekins full of "dip."

 * *The lemon curd can be made up to 1 week ahead and kept refrigerated.*
** *The chips are best served the same day but will stay crisp for up to 2 days.*

chilled passionfruit mousse

Fast, fruity, and cool. I love this dessert all year round: In the summer, the cool, smooth texture makes it refreshing and light. In winter, the citrusy flavor and bright yellow color make it a cheery dessert and a perfect follow-up to a winy stew or chunky soup. Each spoonful should contain a little juice and a little mousse for the best effect.

Passionfruit is so very tangy that I always pair it with something creamy to smooth out the tartness. If you can find 100-percent passionfruit juice, that is the best. If what you find also contains other juices, you can still use it in the recipe—but in that case, eliminate the thawed orange juice concentrate and use an additional ½ cup of the passionfruit juice instead.

MAKES 8 SERVINGS

¾ cup plus 1½ teaspoons passionfruit juice, such as Ceres brand (available at Costco, some supermarkets, and gourmet stores)

½ cup thawed frozen orange juice concentrate

¼ cup plus 2 tablespoons sugar

Scant 1½ teaspoons unflavored dry gelatin

1½ cups heavy cream, whipped

1 orange, juiced

Juice of ½ lemon

½ cup berries, such as raspberries, blueberries, blackberries, or strawberries, or a combination, for garnish

1. In a saucepan, heat the ¾ cup passionfruit juice, the orange juice concentrate, and the sugar over medium-low heat, stirring often until the sugar is dissolved. Meanwhile, in a small bowl, dissolve the gelatin by slowly sprinkling it over 1 tablespoon cold water. Once the gelatin has absorbed the water, add the mixture to the hot juice and stir to melt and combine.

2. Fill a large bowl with ice cubes and cover with cold water. Strain the passionfruit mixture into a smaller bowl and rest the base of the bowl in the ice water. Stir the mixture frequently with a rubber scraper. When it feels cool and just barely begins to set (this will take about 5 minutes), fold in the whipped cream. Pour the mixture into individual serving ramekins, bowls, or glasses (don't fill them all the way; leave ½ inch of space on top) and refrigerate for at least 4 hours. *

3. Just before serving, make the dressing: In a bowl, combine the remaining 1½ teaspoons passionfruit juice, the orange juice, and the lemon juice. Refrigerate until ready to serve.

4. To serve, pour a little bit of dressing (about ⅛ inch deep) into each ramekin, covering the top of the mousse. Garnish with a tablespoon of berries. Serve immediately.

* *The mousses can be refrigerated, covered, for up to 3 days. Make the dressing just before serving.*

cinnamon crème brûlée

As a pastry chef who travels around the country and the world, I have tasted a lot of crème brûlée in my time. Of all possible flavors—from allspice to za'atar—the only one that may be even better than the original is cinnamon. There's something about cinnamon's toasty flavor that picks up the burnt-sugar flavor of the crackly topping. I use enough cinnamon to make the custard quite spicy.

The key is to use very fresh, tasty ground cinnamon. You might think that grinding your own cinnamon from sticks would produce the freshest results, but cinnamon sticks and ground cinnamon actually come from different parts of the cinnamon (cassia) tree. The sticks come from the younger upper branches and have a mild flavor; the pungent ground cinnamon we love is made from chunks of the older, thicker bark near the base of the tree. I buy cinnamon (and learn about it) at Penzeys Spices in Wisconsin, or at *www.penzeys.com*.

MAKES 6 TO 8 SERVINGS

2^1/$_3$ **cups heavy cream**
^{1}/$_3$ **cup half-and-half**
^{1}/$_2$ **vanilla bean, split lengthwise**
^{1}/$_2$ **teaspoon ground cinnamon (see above), or more to taste**

8 large egg yolks
^{1}/$_2$ **cup granulated sugar**
^{1}/$_2$ **cup raw sugar, coarse sugar, or additional granulated sugar, for the topping**

1. Heat the oven to 300 degrees.

2. In a saucepan, heat the cream, half-and-half, vanilla bean, and cinnamon over medium heat just until it comes to a boil. Immediately turn off the heat. Set aside to infuse for 10 minutes.

3. In a large bowl, whisk the egg yolks with the granulated sugar just until combined. Whisking constantly, gradually pour in the hot cream mixture. Strain the mixture into a pitcher to smooth it and to remove the vanilla bean. ✳

4. Pour the mixture into 6 to 8 ovenproof ramekins and arrange in a hot-water bath (see page 23). Bake in the center of the oven until almost set but still slightly jiggly in the center, 30 to 40 minutes. (The custard will finish cooking and set as it cools.) Remove from the water bath and let cool for 15 minutes. Tightly cover each ramekin with plastic wrap, making sure the plastic does not touch the surface of the custard. Refrigerate for at least 2 hours or until ready to serve.**

5. When ready to serve, preheat a broiler to very hot (or fire up your kitchen torch). Uncover the ramekins. To make the sugar coating, pour a thick layer of raw sugar onto the top of one of the custards. Pour off any excess sugar that doesn't stick to the moist surface onto the next custard to create an even thin layer. Repeat until all the custards are coated. Discard any remaining sugar.

6. Place the ramekins on a sheet pan or in a roasting pan and broil until the sugar is melted, caramelized, and well browned, 1 to 2 minutes. Or, zap them one by one with your kitchen torch. Let them cool for 1 minute before serving.

* *The custard mixture can be made up to 3 days before baking and kept refrigerated.*

** *Once baked, the custards can be covered and refrigerated for up to 3 days, but do the topping at the last minute.*

crème caramel

I just love crème caramel, and it's what I always make when I suddenly have to come up with dessert for a party or dinner with friends. The ingredients are all pantry basics—you don't even need heavy cream—and the taste is anything but ordinary. Crème caramel (*flan* in Spanish) has the same fabulous combination of creamy custard and bittersweet burnt sugar tastes as crème brûlée, but it's easier to make. You can infuse almost any flavorings into the milk-and-vanilla mixture: orange rind, cinnamon sticks, chai spices (see page 80), almond extract—whatever you like!

MAKES 8 SERVINGS

3 cups sugar

4 cups whole milk

½ vanilla bean, split lengthwise

4 whole large eggs plus 8 large
  egg yolks

1. Heat the oven to 300 degrees.

2. Pour 2 cups of the sugar into the center of a deep saucepan and set a 9-inch cake pan nearby. Carefully pour ½ cup water around the edge of the sugar, trying not to splash any sugar onto the sides of the pan. Do not stir; gently draw your finger through the center of the sugar twice, making a cross, to moisten it. Over high heat, bring to a boil without stirring. Continue boiling without stirring until golden amber in color, 5 to 10 minutes. Test the color by pouring a few drops on a white plate, keeping in mind that the caramel will continue to cook and darken a bit as it cools. When it reaches the color you want, immediately pour the caramel into the cake pan and swirl to coat the sides (you may want to wear gloves for this). The caramel should go all the way up the sides of the pan. Set the pan aside to cool.*

3. In a saucepan, bring the milk and vanilla bean to a boil over medium heat. Immediately turn off the heat and set aside to infuse. Meanwhile, in a large bowl, whisk together the eggs, additional egg yolks, and the remaining 1 cup sugar. Whisk about ½ cup of the hot milk into the egg mixture. Whisk the remaining hot milk into the egg mixture. Strain the mixture into a pitcher to smooth it and to remove the vanilla bean.** Pour the mixture into the caramel-lined cake pan and place in a hot-water bath (see page 23). Bake in the center of the oven until set in the center, 45 to 50 minutes. Remove from the water bath and let cool. Refrigerate for at least 4 hours before serving.✳✳✳

4. When ready to serve, run a knife around the edges of the dessert. Place a serving platter (choose one deep enough to catch the caramel syrup that will pour out) over the pan, hold them tightly together, and quickly flip them over, then remove the cake pan. Serve in wedges with a bit of the caramel sauce spooned over.

✳ *You can line the pan with caramel and make the custard mixture up to 2 days before baking it.*

✳✳ *Refrigerate them separately, then whisk the custard well and pour it into the pan just before baking (if you are baking the custard right from the refrigerator, add 5 or 10 minutes to the cooking time).*

✳✳✳ *Once baked, the crème caramel can be covered and refrigerated for up to 2 days.*

dried plum and almond
phyllo triangles

Dried plums, toasted nuts, and creamy cheese, all snuggled together in a crisp pastry crust. Dried plums are what we all used to call prunes (and a lot of you still do), but you could also make this recipe with whole dried figs or apricots.

MAKES 16

16 whole pitted dried plums
    (formerly known as prunes)
4 ounces cold cream cheese, cut into
    16 chunks
16 whole almonds, toasted (see
    page 17)

4 sheets frozen phyllo dough, thawed
    in the refrigerator (see page 18)
8 tablespoons (1 stick) unsalted
    butter, melted
2 to 3 tablespoons granulated sugar
Confectioners' sugar, for sprinkling

1. Heat the oven to 375 degrees. Line a sheet pan with nonstick baking mats or parchment paper, or use a heavyweight nonstick sheet pan.

2. Find the opening in each plum (or cut a small opening) and stuff a chunk of cream cheese and an almond inside.

3. Lay a sheet of phyllo on a work surface and brush lightly with melted butter. Sprinkle with granulated sugar. Cut the sheet lengthwise into 3-inch-wide strips. Place a stuffed plum near the end of each strip. Fold one corner of pastry over the plum, making a point at the end of the strip. Then pick up the wrapped plum and flip it over, turning it toward the rest of the strip to enclose the plum in a triangle of phyllo. Keep folding all down the length of the strip, as though folding up a flag, until the plum is wrapped in several layers of phyllo. Place seam side down on the prepared pan. Repeat with the remaining phyllo and plums. Brush all the triangles with melted butter and sprinkle the tops with granulated sugar (you may have a little butter and sugar left over).✱

4. Bake for 10 to 15 minutes, until crisp and light golden brown. Serve warm, sprinkled with confectioners' sugar.

✱ *The assembled triangles can be refrigerated for 3 days. Bake just before serving. If baking right from the refrigerator, you may need to add 5 or 10 minutes to the baking time.*

crisp phyllo cigars with spiced nut filling

This is my spicy version of *baklava* (a classic Greek dessert of phyllo and honey), which I invented for a wedding. I find these little cigars a bit addictive, with their nutty crunch alongside a spicy-sweet syrup. A cup of medium-roast coffee is the perfect pairing.

MAKES 12 TO 16 SERVINGS

For the syrup
1/2 cup sugar
1/2 cup honey
1 cinnamon stick
4 lemon or orange slices, with the peel
    (or use 2 of each)

For the cigars
2 cups finely chopped walnuts or
    pistachios, plus extra for garnish
1 cup sugar
1 1/2 teaspoons ground cardamom
8 tablespoons (1 stick) unsalted butter,
    melted
1 box of phyllo dough, thawed in the
    refrigerator if frozen (see page 18)

1. In a saucepan, combine the syrup ingredients with 1/2 cup water and bring to a boil. Simmer for 5 minutes, cool for 10 minutes, and strain out the aromatics. Set aside.

2. Make the cigars: In a medium bowl, toss together the nuts, sugar, cardamom, and 1 tablespoon of the butter. Butter a 9-inch square baking dish, about 2 inches deep. Unroll the phyllo, cut the stack in half crosswise, and cover with a very lightly dampened towel (keep the phyllo covered as much as possible as you work).

3. Remove 1 sheet of phyllo and place on a work surface. Lightly brush with butter. Lay 1 to 2 tablespoons of the nut mixture along the short side, 1 inch in from the edge of the sheet. Fold the short side over the filling, then roll several times to form a log, enclosing the filling. Twist the ends slightly, like a cigar. Place it in the baking dish. Repeat with the remaining ingredients, snuggling the cigars close together in a single layer in the dish. (You may have some ingredients left over.)*

4. Heat the oven to 350 degrees. Brush all the pastries with butter and bake for 40 minutes. As they come out of the oven, pour the syrup over the pastries and let them soak for at least 1 hour. Sprinkle with chopped nuts.

* You can assemble the entire dish and keep it refrigerated up to 2 days in advance. Bake it the same day it will be served.

kids in the kitchen

If you like to cook—and I know that you do, since you're reading this book—you probably already know that cooking is one of the best activities that kids and grownups can do together. My son, Gio, started showing interest in what I was doing in the kitchen as soon as he could crawl into the room. By the time he was two, he had learned to mix eggs in a bowl. At three, he could crack them open and mix them. At four, he could get them out of the fridge, crack them, mix them, and grate cheese to go on top. Like all little kids, he always loved to "help," and now he really does help me. When there's no school, Gio sometimes comes to work with me and helps by cutting strawberries, rolling cookie dough, stirring ingredients together for *panforte*, or dumping sliced ginger into the stockpot to start a big batch of root beer. We love to cook together, and he loves to "invent" recipes; his latest idea was for a vanilla cake with chocolate frosting! These are some of the lessons I've learned along the way:

* As soon as children are in the kitchen, start teaching them about safety. Your child can learn to be wary of hot burners, sharp knives, and heavy pots. Of course, you should NEVER leave your kids unsupervised in the kitchen, even for a moment.
* Always start with everyone washing hands.
* Baking is a good place for kids to start cooking, since it mostly involves just bowls and spoons, and a parent can handle the oven parts.
* My mantra is: "Everything is washable." Messes will be made, so do what you need to do to control them and not get stressed out. I sometimes put an old shower curtain or other plastic protector on the floor, and even over the whole counter or table when we're doing an especially messy project, like decorating cookies.
* A lot of mixing jobs can be done in big resealable plastic bags instead of bowls. Measure out the ingredients, zip the bag, and a kid can mix, shake, and knead without any mess.
* A standing mixer is especially helpful, since it leaves your hands free to help a child. Also, kids love to watch it go.
* When you are ready to teach them to cut, give your kids soft foods to practice on first: fresh mozzarella cheese, zucchini, the inside of a watermelon. Don't give them rounded fruits and vegetables to cut: Slice them in half first and turn them onto the flat surface to provide a stable base on the cutting board.

* Minimize spills by using high-walled mixing bowls and putting damp kitchen towels underneath them as you mix (this will keep them from sliding around on the counter).
* Give kids small utensils to work with. Measuring spoons, lightweight measuring cups, and small whisks and spatulas will keep them from struggling and spilling. Try to bring the activity down to their level by working on a low table. If you can't bring it down, bring the kids up by always having a step stool or milk crate handy.
* Let the kids decide what flavor the cakes, cookies, or puddings will be. Different extracts, chips, or flavorings are easy ways to mix things up a little. If they're like Gio, they'll enjoy going to the baking aisle of the supermarket to pick out their favorite ingredients.
* Have fun! Make sure the kids taste what they made and help them give it to other appreciative adults to taste. Giving kids cooking skills is such a gift. I know from my own experience that it builds self-esteem and helps them learn about the pleasure of nurturing others. Not to mention the compliments they'll receive!

black and white pudding cups

My favorite way to introduce kids to cooking is to whip up treats that they are used to seeing in packages, such as like Popsicles, ice cream sandwiches, and these pudding cups that are, magically, half chocolate and half vanilla. When you make homemade treats, you don't have to worry about chemical additives or extra salt.

Stirring hot pudding in a saucepan is one of the first jobs I remember performing in my mother's kitchen. And as I now know from my son's Montessori school, cooking helps build self-esteem, fine motor skills, social interaction, and chemistry knowledge (you can illustrate how starch expands in hot liquids). Plus—it's fun!

MAKES 6 TO 8 SERVINGS

4 cups whole, 2% fat, or 1% fat milk

8 large egg yolks

1⅓ cups sugar

6 tablespoons cornstarch

1 teaspoon pure vanilla extract

2 tablespoons cold unsalted butter, cut into pieces

1 ounce unsweetened chocolate, melted (see page 14)

Whipped cream (optional)

1. Set out 6 to 8 ramekins (see page 21) or other cups or small bowls. Cut a piece of smooth plastic (from the lid of a plastic tub of cottage cheese or sherbet, or a take-out container, for example) that will divide the serving cup in half. If using bowls, follow the bottom curve of the bowl when cutting your divider.

2. In a large saucepan, bring the milk to a simmer over medium heat. Immediately turn off the heat. Meanwhile, in a large bowl, whisk the egg yolks and sugar together until smooth and fluffy. Whisk in the cornstarch until completely incorporated. Whisk in a third of the hot milk mixture, then gradually whisk in the rest.

3. Pour the mixture through a fine strainer back into the saucepan to remove any lumps. Whisking constantly, cook over medium heat until thick. When the mixture thickens, the whisk will leave trail marks on the bottom of the pot and the mixture will have a few large bubbles boiling up to the top. Turn off the heat, stir in the vanilla and butter, and whisk until the butter is melted. Pour half of the mixture into a medium bowl and stir in the chocolate until melted and smooth. When cool enough to work with, transfer the warm puddings into separate pastry bags fitted with large plain tips (see page 19) or into thick resealable plastic bags.

4. Stand your plastic divider in a ramekin. If using plastic bags for piping, cut a corner off of each one. Pipe the chocolate pudding on one side of the plastic, then the vanilla on the other. Pull out the plastic, put it in another ramekin, and repeat. Tap the ramekins on the counter a few times to settle the puddings. Refrigerate the ramekins until ready to serve. (If you like pudding skin, do not cover them. If you don't like it, cover them tightly with plastic wrap.) Refrigerate for at least 2 hours.✱ Serve cold with a dollop of whipped cream, if desired.

✱ *Covered and refrigerated, the puddings will last for up to 3 days.*

chocolate–cranberry graham cracker bars

These crunchy bars are based on a "praline" recipe I learned in my summer-camp baking class. Like s'mores, they were probably invented by some clever cook at the Nabisco company in order to get kids eating more graham crackers. It worked on me! I've also tried these out on my son's classmates, and they love making and eating them every time. Parents seem to like them too; the chewy dried cranberries add a tangy touch.

MAKES 16 BARS

12 whole graham crackers, broken into $\frac{1}{2}$-inch to 1-inch pieces (you can do this in a sealed plastic bag to control the crumbs)
$\frac{3}{4}$ cup dried cranberries

12 tablespoons ($1\frac{1}{2}$ sticks) salted butter
$\frac{3}{4}$ cup light brown sugar
6 ounces semisweet chocolate, chopped (see page 15)

1. Heat the oven to 350 degrees.

2. Combine the graham cracker pieces and the cranberries in an 8-inch square baking pan. Combine the butter and brown sugar in a saucepan, bring to a boil, and boil for 2 minutes. Pour the hot brown sugar mixture over the graham crackers and toss to coat well. Bake for 10 minutes.

3. As the pan comes out of the oven, sprinkle the chocolate evenly over the surface. The warmth of the crust will melt the chocolate. Set aside at room temperature to cool until the chocolate is firm, at least 1 hour. Cut into small bars and store in an airtight container.*

* *The bars will stay crisp and tasty for up to a week.*

no-clean-up
cinnamon-raisin bread

I Love Resealable Plastic Bags. I find them so handy as pastry bags, for crushing candy canes or nuts, as freezer containers for egg whites and cookie dough . . . the list never seems to end. But I had never thought of using them as a painless way to mix bread until I helped my son's first-grade teacher, Mrs. Bricker, bake in class. Instead of kneading on a floured surface—which means a completely floured kitchen—we did all the mixing and kneading inside a big plastic bag. Their hands stayed clean—and the kitchen did too!

MAKES 1 LOAF

1 package (1/4 ounce) active dry yeast
3 cups all-purpose flour, plus extra as needed
2 tablespoons sugar
1 teaspoon salt

1 teaspoon ground cinnamon
2 tablespoons unsalted butter, at room temperature
1 cup warm water
1/2 cup raisins

1. Put the yeast, 1½ cups of the flour, the sugar, salt, and cinnamon into a 1-gallon thick, resealable plastic bag and seal it. Shake to blend the dry ingredients. Add the butter and water and seal the bag again. Knead the dough by squeezing and squishing the bag with your hands, blending the ingredients until they are well mixed. Open the bag, add 1½ cups more flour, and seal it. Continue kneading until the dough is almost smooth. Add the raisins and work them in. Knead in more flour (if necessary) to make a dough that is smooth and springy but not sticky. Let the dough rest in the bag at room temperature for 1 hour.

2. Open the bag (leave the dough inside) and press the dough down until it's almost flat. Remove the dough from the bag and roll it into a thick log the length of a loaf pan, about 9 inches. Butter the loaf pan and place the dough in it. Place the pan in the plastic bag and seal it. Let the dough rise in the bag in a warm spot (such as a turned-off oven) until doubled in size, 1 hour to 90 minutes.

3. Heat the oven to 375 degrees. Remove the pan from the bag and bake for 25 to 30 minutes, until golden brown. Remove the bread from the pan immediately.✳

✳ *The bread will last for up to a week at room temperature and freezes well.*

killer buttermilk biscuits

I've tried out a lot of biscuit recipes, and this one, adapted from brilliant cooking teacher Shirley Corriher (who gave me my first bag of White Lily flour), is my new favorite. They are just as tasty as whipped-cream biscuits, but quicker and easier to make. You get to skip the step of rolling and cutting out the dough: Just scoop it into balls with an ice-cream scoop, roll them in flour, and pack them into a pan. Kids are very good at this.

White Lily, popular for biscuits in the South, is a very finely ground flour, made from "soft" wheat (pasta is made from "hard" wheat, and all-purpose flour is a combination of the two). You can order it online from *www.whitelily.com.* These would make a stunning breakfast (or dessert!) with butter and honey or homemade Plum Jam (page 125).

MAKES ABOUT 10 BISCUITS

3 cups White Lily flour or all-purpose flour
1½ teaspoons baking powder
⅛ teaspoon baking soda
½ teaspoon salt

2 tablespoons sugar
¼ cup vegetable shortening
⅔ cup half-and-half
1 cup buttermilk

1. Heat the oven to 425 degrees. Butter an 8- or 9-inch round cake or pie pan.

2. Combine 2 cups of the flour and the other dry ingredients in the bowl of a mixer fitted with a paddle attachment. Add the shortening and mix until some pea-sized pieces of shortening remain. Using a wooden spoon, stir in the half-and-half and buttermilk and let sit for 2 minutes. The dough should be very wet and look like cottage cheese.

3. Spread out the remaining cup of flour on a large plate and flour your hands. Using a medium ice-cream scoop, drop a few scoopfuls of batter onto the flour. Using your hands, gently turn and toss the scoops of batter in the flour until coated. Lift the biscuits out and arrange them around the edge of the buttered cake or pie pan, packing them in snugly. Repeat, filling in the center of the pan with more biscuits.

4. Bake in the center of the oven for 15 to 20 minutes. Break the biscuits apart and serve hot. *

* Biscuits always taste best if they're mixed, baked, and eaten right away.

cookieburgers

My friend Mary Mullins brought these silly but tasty treats to a backyard barbecue one summer. They really look like tiny hamburgers. Obviously, they are great for kids' parties, especially during grilling season. To get the biggest laugh, serve them next to shot glasses filled with strawberry malteds.

Vanilla wafer cookies vary in flavor; I find the tastiest ones are from Keebler and Nabisco.

MAKES 15

30 vanilla wafer cookies
1 cup thick chocolate frosting
(store-bought is fine)

1 tube each of green, yellow,
and red frosting

Using the vanilla wafer cookies as the bun, build a hamburger by spreading a thick (at least ⅛ inch) layer of chocolate frosting on the flat side of half the cookies (the burger). On top of the chocolate, pipe thick wavy green lines for lettuce, red squiggles for ketchup, and yellow squiggles for mustard. Do this close to the edges to make sure they will be visible when you place the second cookie on top. Finish the "burgers" by placing the remaining cookies on top.✲

✲ *The cookies can be stored in an airtight container (in the refrigerator if the weather is hot) for up to 1 day.*

peanut butter worms

These are fun to make with kids, and quite nutritious compared to many treats. You can make almost any shapes out of this pliable mixture of peanut butter and powdered milk; it holds together very well. If it gets sticky as you work, chill it for a little while or add a little more confectioners' sugar.

When I made these worms for Gio's bug-themed birthday party, I fitted a small plate inside the top of a flowerpot and filled it to the top with chocolate cake crumbs, to look like dirt. Then we made it look like the worms were crawling out of the dirt. It looked totally gross, of course, and all the kids loved it. You can also coil up the worms and make a few snails, using short lengths of black licorice strings as the antennae.

MAKES ABOUT 2 DOZEN

1 cup smooth peanut butter
$1/2$ cup honey
$1^1/2$ cups dry milk powder
$1/2$ cup confectioners' sugar
Whole raisins, currants, and/or halved peanuts

1. Combine the peanut butter and honey in a food processor or mixer and mix well. Add the dry milk powder and the confectioners' sugar and mix again until smooth and well blended.

2. Turn out onto a work surface and gather the mixture into one long log. Pull off a small handful and roll into a thick worm, about the thickness of a finger. Decorate with two raisins, currants, or peanut halves at one end to look like eyes. Transfer to a tray and repeat with the remaining peanut butter mixture. Chill for at least 30 minutes before serving. Store in an airtight container.✳

✳ *The worms can be refrigerated for up to 1 day before eating.*

snickerdoodles

This is a classic recipe from my grandmother Elsie, though I assume they hand this recipe out to all grandmothers as part of their initiation. I've always loved the crackly sugar coating, and I remember helping her roll the dough balls in the cinnamon sugar. Some sources say that the name is German or Dutch, others that it's a nonsense word invented in America. If you know for sure, you can E-mail or write to me at the Food Network: *www.foodnetwork.com*!

These make a great holiday dessert served with Pumpkin Pots (page 38).

MAKES ABOUT 3 DOZEN

For the cookie dough
3½ **cups all-purpose flour**
1 **tablespoon baking powder**
2 **teaspoons baking soda**
¼ **teaspoon ground cinnamon**
1 **cup (2 sticks) salted butter, softened**
2 **cups sugar**

2 **large eggs**
2½ **teaspoons pure vanilla extract**

For the topping
3 **tablespoons sugar**
½ **teaspoon ground cinnamon**

1. Make the dough: Stir the dry ingredients together. In a mixer fitted with the paddle attachment, cream the butter. Mix in the sugar, then add the eggs and vanilla and mix thoroughly. Add the dry ingredients and mix until blended. If the dough seems sticky, gather into a ball and refrigerate for 1 hour.

2. Heat the oven to 375 degrees. Roll the dough into walnut-sized balls.*

3. Make the topping: In a small bowl, stir together the sugar and cinnamon. Roll each ball in cinnamon sugar until well coated. Place on an ungreased sheet pan, spacing them 2 inches apart. If desired, flatten the cookies slightly with the bottom of a drinking glass (some people like a flatter cookie, and kids like to do it).

4. Bake for 10 to 12 minutes, until the cookies are puffed up and the surface is slightly cracked. Let cool on the pan for a few minutes, then remove to a wire rack to cool completely. Store in an airtight container.

* *The dough balls can be frozen in a resealable plastic bag for up to 2 weeks. Thaw at room temperature for 15 minutes, then roll in cinnamon sugar and bake. You may need to increase the baking time by 5 minutes.*

katie's pinwheel cookies

These pinwheel-shaped cookies are so very pretty—and easy—that I've adapted them to every possible holiday. My friend Mary Douglas and her daughter Katie brought them to a Fourth-of-July party and I immediately begged for the recipe. I do a lot of experimenting with different colored sugars, and you can too! Using red sugar with green centers works well to make Christmas cookies that look like poinsettias.

   Since each cookie has plenty of sugar on top, I find that the cookie dough itself doesn't need any sweetening at all. You can make the dough and cut the squares in advance, then save the decorating step for the kids.

MAKES 30

12 tablespoons (1½ sticks) unsalted
   butter, softened
8 ounces cream cheese, softened
1 large egg, separated
2 cups all-purpose flour
1 tablespoon baking powder

30 wooden popsicle-type sticks
   (available at craft stores and large
   stores like Target)
1 cup colored sugar (see above)
About 30 M &M candies

1. In a mixer fitted with a paddle attachment, beat the butter, cream cheese, and egg yolk together until smooth. Mix in the flour and baking powder. Mix until blended and form into a disk. Wrap in plastic wrap and refrigerate for 1 hour.*

2. Divide the dough in half. On a lightly floured surface, roll half of the dough into a 15 × 9-inch rectangle. Return the remaining dough to the refrigerator. With the tip of a sharp knife or a pizza cutter, trim any uneven edges and cut the rectangle into 3-inch squares. Place the squares 1½ inches apart on ungreased sheet pans.**

3. Heat the oven to 350 degrees.

4. Lightly whisk the egg white and brush one dough square all over with egg white. Lightly press the top 1½ inches of a wooden stick into the lower half of the square (see photo). Using a sharp knife, cut the dough diagonally from each corner to within ½ inch of the center of the square (see photo).

5. Sprinkle 1 teaspoon colored sugar evenly over the whole square. Fold in every other point of the square to the center, forming a pinwheel, overlapping the corners at the center and pressing them down gently to seal (see photo). Press an M & M in the center of the pinwheel, covering the folded-in points. Repeat with the remaining squares.

6. Bake for 9 to 12 minutes, until dry and very light golden. Store the finished cookies between layers of wax paper in an airtight container.***

* *The dough can be mixed and kept refrigerated for up to 2 days.*

** *Or, you can refrigerate it for 1 hour, then do the rolling and cutting, then store the squares between sheets of wax paper, refrigerated, for up to 2 days or frozen for up to 2 weeks.*

*** *Once baked, the cookies will stay crisp and tasty for about 4 days.*

caramel corn with {salted peanuts and dried cherries

This is what I call real Chicago regional cuisine. Cracker Jack was invented in Chicago in 1893. I have loved it forever, so this is my salty-sweet, crunchy-chewy tribute. The best toy surprise I ever got was a miniature blue toaster with a piece of plastic toast popping out. I still have it in my collection of "play food."

I use small, hull-less Black Diamond kernels, as I really do find that it makes the tastiest popcorn. To pop corn properly, pour a layer of kernels in a heavy-bottomed large pot and add just enough vegetable oil to cover. Put the lid on and cook on high until you hear the first pop. Immediately take it off the heat and let it sit for 1 minute. Then return it to the heat and finish popping, shaking the pan the whole time. I don't know exactly why this works so well, but this is what my dad does and his popcorn is always the best.

MAKES 6 TO 8 SERVINGS

2 cups sugar

1 tablespoon butter

6 cups popped corn, homemade (see above) or store-bought

$\frac{1}{2}$ cup toasted salted peanuts

$\frac{1}{2}$ cup dried cherries

1. Pour the sugar into the center of a deep, heavy saucepan. Carefully pour $\frac{2}{3}$ cup water around the walls of the pan, trying not to splash any sugar onto the walls. Do not stir; gently draw your finger twice through the center of the sugar, making a cross, to moisten it. Over high heat, bring to a full boil and cook without stirring until golden brown in color, 10 to 15 minutes. Toward the end, swirl the mixture occasionally (by tilting the pot) to even out the color. Turn off the heat and stir in the butter, then the popcorn, peanuts, and cherries.

2. Pour out the mixture onto a nonstick sheet pan or a pan lined with a nonstick baking mat. Let it cool for a few minutes, until just cool enough to touch. As soon as you can, start breaking the mixture up into clusters, working quickly so that you finish before the mixture cools too much. Let cool to room temperature and store in an airtight container.*

* The caramel corn will keep well for up to 1 week.

caramel peanut suckers

These are the easiest lollipops in the world—toothsome lumps of caramel sprinkled with peanuts. They came from my love for taffy apples, my favorite childhood autumn treat, but are a lot simpler. After all, when it comes to taffy apples, isn't the taffy the point, not the apple?

In the Chicago area, the Affy Tapple company has pretty much cornered the market. Each fall, you can visit the factory and see the production line turn out thousands of taffy apples. One year in grade school, my entrepreneurial childhood friend Lauren Shay bought a whole box of Affy Tapples and sold them for 25 cents apiece out on the playground at recess.

MAKES 12

1¼ cups sugar
1½ tablespoons unsalted butter
¼ cup heavy cream, warmed
½ cup chopped peanuts or chopped
    semisweet chocolate

12 pointed wooden skewers, about
    6 inches long

1. Pour the sugar into the center of a deep saucepan. Carefully pour ⅓ cup water around the walls of the pan, trying not to splash any sugar onto the walls. Do not stir; gently draw your finger twice through the center of the sugar, making a cross, to moisten it. Over high heat, bring to a full boil and cook without stirring until amber caramel in color, 5 to 10 minutes. Immediately turn off the heat and use a wooden spoon to stir in the butter. Slowly stir in the cream (it will bubble up and may splatter) and the peanuts. Let cool slightly to thicken.

2. Butter a sheet pan very well. Pour the caramel onto the pan and spread it out to the corners. Let it cool until slightly firmed but still pliable enough to roll into balls (start checking it after about 40 minutes). Using the tip of a sharp knife, cut the caramel into 1½- to 2-inch squares. Roll each square in your hands into a ball. Push a skewer into the center of the ball. Let the suckers set at room temperature until firm.*

* These suckers are best served the same day, but they can be stacked in an airtight container, with wax paper between the layers, for up to 3 days.

frozen milk chocolate pops

Why buy these when they're so easy to make? And kids can do it all by themselves (almost); you'll probably have to clean up the counter afterward. I still love the flavor of chocolate milk, and I often indulge in these treats in the summer—it's a quick, cold chocolate fix.

You can buy popsicle molds at specialty cookware shops, or during the summer at large stores like Target and Wal-Mart.

MAKES 8

3 cups milk

1/2 heaping cup chocolate milk
    powder (such as Nesquik)

2 tablespoons malted milk powder
    (such as Carnation)

2 tablespoons light corn syrup

Combine all the ingredients in a blender and blend well. Pour into a popsicle mold and insert wooden sticks, then freeze until hard, at least 1 day.

* *The frozen pops will last for up to a week.*

*index